Programming for School-Age Child Care

PROGRAMMING FOR SCHOOL-AGE CHILD CARE

A Children's Literature Based Guide

A15042 703295

MELBA HAWKINS

1987
LIBRARIES UNLIMITED, INC.
Littleton, Colorado

Copyright © Melba Hawkins
All Rights Reserved
Printed in the United States of America

No part of this publication may be reproduced, stored in a retrieval system, or transmitted, in any form or by any means, electronic, mechanical, photocopying, recording, or otherwise, without the prior written permission of the publisher.

LIBRARIES UNLIMITED, INC.
P.O. Box 263
Littleton, Colorado 80160-0263

Library of Congress Cataloging-in-Publication Data

Hawkins, Melba.
  Programming for school-age child care.

  Bibliography: p. 107
  Includes index.
  1. School-age child care--Activity programs.
2. Children's literature--Study and teaching.
3. Children--Books and reading. I. Title. [DNLM:
1. Child Care. 2. Child Day Care Centers--standards.
3. Child Development. 4. Literature. 5. Play and
Playthings. 6. Teaching Materials. WS 105.5.P5 H394p]
HQ778.6.H38 1987   016.81'08'09282   87-4017
ISBN 0-87287-555-5 (lib. bdg.)

Libraries Unlimited books are bound with Type II nonwoven material that meets and exceeds National Association of State Textbook Administrators' Type II nonwoven material specifications Class A through E.

CONTENTS

Introduction ix

1 PROGRAMMING FOR SCHOOL-AGE CHILD CARE 1
    Developmental Characteristics of School-Age Children 1
        Five-Year-Olds 1
        Six-Year-Olds 2
        Seven-Year-Olds 2
        Eight-Year-Olds 2
    Developmental Tasks of School-Age Children 2
    Assessing Individual Interests 3
    Responsive Programming for School-Age Child Care 5
        Program Models for Out-of-School Care 5
        Schedule and Activities 6
        Facilities and Activities 6
        Staff 8
        Field Trips 8
    Management and Group Size 8
    Rationale for Children's Literature Based Programming 9
    General Objectives 10
        Creative Art Activities 11
        Creative Dramatics 11
        Music Activities 11
        Cooking Experiences 11
        Celebrations 11
    Uses of the School-Age Programming Guide 11
    Unit Planning 13
    Notes 15

2 LET'S CREATE: Children's Literature and Creative Art Activities 16
    Values of Using Literature Based Creative Art Activities 16
    Techniques for Creative Art Activities 17
    Methods of Evaluation 17
    Children's Literature and Art Activities 17
    Notes 38

3 LET'S PRETEND: Children's Literature and Creative Dramatics....................39
   Values of Using Literature Based Creative Dramatic Activities..................39
   Techniques for Creative Dramatic Activities...........................40
   Kinds of Literature for Dramatization.................................40
   Methods of Evaluation..41
   Children's Literature and Creative Dramatics.........................41
      Bible Stories..41
      Fables...42
      Folk Tales and Fairy Tales.......................................42
      Nursery Rhymes...44
      Children's Picture Book Stories..................................44

4 LET'S MAKE MUSIC: Children's Literature and Creative Music Activities..............48
   Values of Using Literature Based Creative Music Activities..................48
   Techniques for Creative Music Activities..............................48
   Kinds of Literature to Use with Music.................................49
   Methods of Evaluation...49
   Children's Literature and Creative Music Activities...................49
      Picture Books of Single Songs....................................49
      Children's Books Involving Instruments and Sound Effects.........53
      Using Music as an Extension of Children's Picture Book Stories...55
   Notes..58

5 LET'S COOK: Children's Literature and Cooking Experiences....................59
   Values of Using Literature Based Cooking Experiences..................59
   Techniques for Cooking Activities.....................................60
   Methods of Evaluation...60
   Children's Literature and Cooking Experiences.........................60
      Nursery Rhymes...72
   Notes..75

6 LET'S CELEBRATE: Children's Literature and Special Days of the Year..............76
   Values of Using Literature Based Activities for Special Days of the Year................76
   Techniques for Celebrating with Children's Literature.................77
   Methods of Evaluation...77
   Children's Literature and Special Days of the Year....................77
      January..77
      February...84
      March..87
      April..88
      May..91
      June...92
      July...93
      August...94
      September..95
      October..97
      November...99
      December...100
   Notes..106

7 RESOURCES: A Selected Annotated Bibliography 107
    General 107
    Selection Tools for Children's Literature 109
    Periodicals 109
    School-Age Child Care Administration and Programming 110
    Art Activities 113
    Creative Dramatics 114
    Music 115
    Cooking 115
    Special Day Celebrations 116

Index 119

INTRODUCTION

In most communities, today, there is a growing need for school-age child care, care for children away from home while parents work and school is not in session. Appropriate programming for school-age child care is becoming an increasing concern. The purpose of this guide is to present children's literature based ideas for school-age child care programming. The target age group is children in kindergarten through third grade, or five- through eight-year-olds.

A review of the literature in the child care field reveals an increase in resources for teachers and librarians suggesting activities for children that will extend their experiences with and responses to literature. One also finds many resources for games, arts and crafts activities, music, and creative dramatic ideas. However, very few resources deal directly with programming suggestions for school-age child care. This guide specifically addresses the need for programming ideas for school-age child care by providing a number of children's literature based activities. These ideas may be used independently or in combination with others for school-age child care programming. The use of many recent titles in children's literature, and the resource section for teachers and librarians, also make this guide unique.

THE NEED FOR SCHOOL-AGE CHILD CARE

The need for school-age child care has increased dramatically in recent years. The traditional belief that once a child enters school he/she no longer needs child care arrangements just does not exist. In *Half a Childhood: Time for School-Age Child Care* the authors emphasize that indeed at least half or more of one's childhood is spent outside the school.[1] An increasing number of parents each year are seeking appropriate programs away from home for their school-age children, before and after school and during school holidays.

Nationally, over 60 percent of mothers with children ages six to thirteen work outside the home. This percentage is predicted to become even higher within the next few years. Mothers are in the labor force either by choice or necessity or both. Societal changes have also influenced the need for school-age child care. Not only are more mothers working, but more are single parents. Family mobility has presented another problem. The extended family and reliable neighborhood child care arrangements are not the options they have been in the past.

Schools operate approximately six hours per day; however, a parent's work day is much longer. What do parents and their children do about the hours before and after school and the long days during school holidays and summer vacations?

x / INTRODUCTION

A survey in most communities will reveal the gamut of arrangements. Background studies in preparation for the School Facilities Child Care Act (Senate Bill S1531) showed that approximately six million "latchkey" children between the ages of six and thirteen take care of themselves when they return home from school.[2] In most cases these "latchkey" arrangements are not the first choice of the working parents, but the only alternative. Many children go home to watch television, not allowed to leave the house until a parent comes home from work. Others are cared for by older siblings or check in with neighbors or a baby-sitter while some children are forced to fend for themselves in the neighborhood until a parent comes home to unlock the door. Some children participate in and float from various community programs such as the public library and recreation and craft centers to fill up their afternoons and days.

Especially younger school-age children, generally children under fifth grade, should not be left alone on a regular, extended basis. Children who do not have proper adult supervision day after day during these in-between hours tend to have a variety of problems including unhealthy fears, emotional upsets, loneliness, poor nutritional habits, and limited opportunities for physical exercise to mention a few.[3] Safety is another primary concern. Opportunities for social interaction and development are also limited for "latchkey" children. As a general rule, care by an older sibling is not an ideal arrangement either as premature responsibility is placed on both children.

Another problem with "latchkey" arrangements is the concern they generate for parents. Mothers begin to worry and their productivity level tends to decrease as the time for children to be at home alone occurs. Children calling to check in with parents at work is more acceptable in some work settings than others.

Recognizing the rights of children to supervision, guidance, companionship, and a safe environment, parents and community leaders are responding to the need for school-age child care. As proposed in the School Facilities Child Care Act, many schools are becoming involved in extended-day or school based programs to meet the child care needs of their students. In most communities, however, the school based programs, if they exist at all, serve only a small number of the students who need child care and most of these programs do not operate when the schools are closed for holidays.

Other options to parents might be a neighborhood family day care arrangement, private child care center programs, and recreational programs sponsored by such organizations as local recreation departments, YMCA, YWCA, and Girls' and Boys' Clubs. An increasing variety of programs for school-age children may be found in some communities, while in others such programs are essentially nonexistent. The challenge is to provide program options for school-age children and their parents.

What are the qualities of a good school-age child care program? This is a question parents ask as they look for a program for their children and a question school-age child care providers should ask as they evaluate their programs.

Good programs for school-age children not only provide a safe, secure physical environment, but also meet children's developmental needs and individual needs and interests. Good school-age child care programs also take into account children's family situations and cultural backgrounds. A school-age child care program should be an enriching program that complements and supplements the home and school but does not try to duplicate or take the place of either. Good school-age child care programming not only takes into account the child's needs, interests and background, but also a good understanding of his/her school experiences.

This guide deals briefly with the developmental needs of five- through eight-year-olds, the need and techniques for interest assessment, and the components of responsive programming for school-age children. The three program models—child centered, adult centered, and unit based—are discussed. A good school-age child care program includes components of all three models to meet the needs of the total child: his/her social, emotional, physical, intellectual, and moral/spiritual development; and his/her individual interests.

Although the unit/theme based approach to programming can be supported by the use of children's literature, very few programming resources specifically for school-age child care exist. Activities in such areas as art, creative dramatics, music, cooking, games, recreation, field trips, creative writing, and science can serve as extensions of the literature. The chapters in this guide include literature based activities in art, creative dramatics, music, and cooking, as well as a combination of suggestions for special celebrations.

The guide is divided into the following chapters: "Let's Create," "Let's Pretend," "Let's Make Music," "Let's Cook," and "Let's Celebrate." Each chapter states values and techniques for using the suggested activities as extensions of the selected children's literature. Means of evaluation and resources for teachers in each area are presented. A selected, annotated bibliography of resources for teachers specifically related to children's literature, school-age child care, and the art, creative dramatics, music, cooking, and special days activities is included at the end of the guide. This bibliography provides a unique source for school-age child care practitioners planning programs and activities for the children with whom they work. The children's literature is indexed by subject, author/illustrator, and title for easy access for unit or theme planning.

This guide is intended to provide practical ideas for teachers and librarians involved in school-age child care programs. It is hoped that teachers and librarians will add their own ideas as they develop their programs, use titles accessible to them, and find new titles. The ideas need not be limited to child care programs. Teachers in public school kindergarten through third grade and school librarians planning programs to involve and extend children's experiences with their literature will also find this guide useful.

The whole premise of the suggestions in this guide is that children learn by doing, that play is their work, and that many experiences with their literature is important. They need to be actively involved in appropriate aspects of the world around them and need many opportunities to develop this sense of competence to effectively function in their world. An old Chinese proverb seems to summarize very well the reasons for planning and providing literature related experiences for school-age children.

The proverb says:

> I hear, and I forget.
> I see, and I remember.
> I do, and I understand.

HAPPY READING AND CREATING!

NOTES

[1] Judith Bender, Charles H. Flatter, and Barbara Schuyler-Haas Elder, *Half a Childhood: Time for School-Age Child Care* (Nashville, Tenn.: School-Age Notes, Inc., 1984), 11.

[2] "Administrative Notes: School Facilities Child Care Act," *School Age Notes* 4 (January/February 1984): 10.

[3] Lynette Long and Thomas Long, *The Handbook for Latchkey Children and Their Parents* (New York: Arbor House, 1983), 10-12.

1
PROGRAMMING FOR SCHOOL-AGE CHILD CARE

This chapter addresses the developmental characteristics of school-age children in several age categories. Assessing children's individual interests and developing responsive programming for their care are also discussed.

The rationale for the use of children's literature as a basis for school-age child care programming is presented. Suggestions for how school-age child care teachers, children's librarians, and classroom teachers can use the literature based ideas are also given.

DEVELOPMENTAL CHARACTERISTICS OF SCHOOL-AGE CHILDREN

Effective programming for school-age child care is based on a sound understanding of the needs of the whole child providing opportunities for the best social, emotional, physical, intellectual, and moral/spiritual development. Although no two children are exactly alike and development, interests, and abilities vary from child to child, children do go through similar stages of development. Understanding these general characteristics and what to expect is important in planning for school-age children. Each year of ages five through eight, and general characteristics of the age, are presented in the following section. Programming ideas in this guide are suggested for children ages five through eight.

Five-Year-Olds

Five-year-olds are active, have short attention spans, and need many opportunities to make choices to participate in firsthand experiences. They tire easily and usually need a rest or quiet time during the day. They are developing a good vocabulary, ask lots of questions, and are becoming excited about words and what they say. Five-year-olds take peer approval and disapproval very seriously. They like group games for a short time, but a lot of rules and competition are hard for them to handle because they do not like to lose. Although they need loving, caring adults on whom to depend, they are becoming independent, like to do things for themselves, and feel proud of special jobs in which they can help at home and school. Play is five-year-olds' work. They like to pretend and interact with their friends. Real facts and realistic stories interest them; and, although they like to pretend, they are beginning to distinguish between fact and fantasy.

Six-Year-Olds

The six-year-old takes pride in being in first grade and in the intellectual skills he is developing. Growth is slow and steady at this age. Six-year-olds are active and need opportunities for running, jumping, chasing, and other active games and activities. They like make-believe and pretend play, like play with peers, especially small groups of friends of the same sex. They like jokes, rhymes, and experimenting with words. They like to play games and to make up their own rules, but are quick to protest when others cheat. Six-year-olds are literal minded, concerned about realistic things, and enjoy the use of real tools and materials.

Seven-Year-Olds

Seven is a sensitive age. Most seven-year-olds think and talk about their feelings. They like to play in large groups although they need time with a few special friends and time alone. Peer approval and conformity to the group are important at this age; they like to dress like their friends and do what they do. They like to play in secret hideaways, out of the sight of adults. Following the rules and concerns about good and bad, right and wrong, are important at this age. Seven-year-olds are moody; sometimes they like to run errands and help others and sometimes they do not. They are able to read independently if the words are not too hard. Sometimes they want to make and do things that are too hard. This is a critical age for adults to provide encouragement and support to help children feel successful and competent. Seven-year-olds still have a need for activity and like to jump rope, play hopscotch and jacks, and participate in active games.

Eight-Year-Olds

At eight, friends, especially "best friends" of the same sex, are very important. Children at this age like group projects, group games with rules, and clubs. They enjoy games that use small muscles like jacks and darts and active activities like riding a bicycle and roller skating. Although they often test their limits with adults, eight-year-olds like real conversations with adults. They like to learn about real things and use real tools and materials. They are often involved in special interest activities, hobbies, and collections. This is the age that many children become interested in the past, what happened long ago or in "olden times." Eight-year-olds are able to do many things for themselves and need opportunity to become involved appropriately in the world around them.

In summary, Erik Erikson labels the five-year-old as generally in the stage of "initiative versus guilt." The five-year-old and young six-year-old explore the physical world with their senses and their social and physical worlds with questions, reasoning, imagination, and creative powers. Through curiosity, questioning, and firsthand experiences, they learn about the world around them and begin to see their place in this world.

The years beginning around age seven Erikson calls the stage of "industry versus inferiority." At this stage according to Erikson, developmental tasks include acquiring a sense of industry or a desire for producing things, a developing sense of competence both physically and intellectually, and the fending off of a sense of inferiority. This age child needs to experience successes that he and others can recognize.[1]

DEVELOPMENTAL TASKS OF SCHOOL-AGE CHILDREN

The developmental tasks of a school-age child are specific. He needs to continue the development of a positive self-concept with an increasing need to develop competence, skills, and concepts necessary for everyday living. These skills include the fundamentals in reading, writing, and calculating. The tasks of laying foundations toward personal independence and skills for positive, self-confident social interactions are important. Experiences in the community and with acceptable adult models to assist in learning appropriate masculine and feminine social roles and attitudes toward social groups and institutions are also important.

ASSESSING INDIVIDUAL INTERESTS

A background knowledge of general developmental needs and tasks of school-age children, coupled with a strong understanding of the individual needs and interests of the children the program is to serve, provides a basis for effective programming for school-age child care. There are many ways of assessing children's interests, informally and formally.

Informally one discovers children's interests by observation of their play and other activities, and through conversation and their inquiries. Parents are also important resources in identifying children's interests. Through the initial interview or a brief questionnaire, parents can quickly identify some of a child's interests and talents.

More formal means of determining interests are periodic interviews with nonreaders or paper and pencil questionnaires for readers. Nonreaders might also draw pictures of what they like to do or what they like or dislike. Group discussions are very useful in assessing individual and group interests.

In an interest interview ask the child such questions as:

- What do you like to do more than anything else?
- What do you like best about school?
- What do you not like about school?
- What do you like to do after school? on weekends? during the summer?
- When you are bored, what do you like to do?
- What is your favorite food?
- Do you have a favorite book or story? What is it?
- What TV programs do you like best?
- What are your hobbies?
- What would you like to do in the after school (school holiday) program?

Interviews should be kept brief and should be done frequently to keep current on children's changing interests.

At the beginning of a new year, children might be encouraged to do get acquainted interviews. One child will ask another questions about him/herself, and what he/she likes to do. School-age children enjoy using tape recorders and this is a good way for them to record responses. Teachers could also record interviews with children.

Individual interests are assessed as teachers conduct group planning sessions. During a group planning session, discuss holidays, events, and community activities coming up. Ask children what they like to do for leisure and for fun. Have children suggest things they would like to do during the school-age child care program. As a group, eliminate suggestions that are not possible due to expense, location, elements of safety, or general feasibility. Accept ideas that are possible and encourage children to help prioritize them. One way for children to be specific in what they would like to do is to provide a chart with possible activities and allow children to sign up for their choices. For kindergarten and first graders, charts with pictures and words are necessary. Care must be given to respect children's sincere ideas even if they cannot be used. In the course of the time the group is together, make a point of responding to each child's ideas and expressed interests in some way so he will realize that his ideas are recognized and that his input will make a difference.

The paper and pencil questionnaire (see figure 1.1) is an example of an interest assessment for children who read and write.

All About ME

1. My name is _____.

2. I am _____ years old.

3. I am in the _____ grade.

4. My favorite food is _____.

5. At school I like _____
   _____ best of all.

6. My favorite teacher is _____
   because _____.

7. After school I like to _____.

8. When I am bored, I like to _____.

9. The book or story I like best is _____
   _____.

10. The TV program I like best is _____.

11. My hobbies are _____.

12. I need _____.

Fig. 1.1.

Questions about vacation activities and other specific events and holidays might be included in an interest survey. Care must be taken to make the questionnaire brief. If interest interviews or surveys are used, teachers must then have a plan to use this information and in some way respond to expressed interests of each child.

The most effective needs assessment is a combination of both the formal and informal techniques. Needs assessments must be done frequently for children's interests change as they grow and develop and have new experiences at home and at school. Teachers should also take advantage of opportunities to encourage the development of new interests by providing a variety of materials, experiences, attention getting bulletin boards and displays, and resource persons for the children in their programs.

RESPONSIVE PROGRAMMING FOR SCHOOL-AGE CHILD CARE

Responsive programming for school-age child care considers out-of-school time as one of children's most precious commodities.[2] The time is valuable time for children to have enriching experiences, to practice foundational skills necessary for future independence, to use many of the concepts they are learning in school, to develop competence and self-confidence, and to pursue individual interests. When a school-age child care program supplements the school, it provides opportunities for children to develop motor skills, to engage in many activities for creative expression, and to develop social skills. The program complements the home by being more like home than the formal school situation in that it gives children experiences with self-help skills by providing real tools and materials, choices of activities, one to one relationships, and a homelike atmosphere.

Program Models for Out-of-School Care

A review of the literature supports the summary of Schofield and Shaw that identifies three basic program models.[3] These program models are the child centered, adult centered, and unit based models.

The first model, the child centered approach, employs the idea that children be free to choose their activities with the adult assuming the roles of resource and prop person. The second model is the adult centered approach, a more structured activity based program with high adult direction. This model includes recreational and tutorial programs.

The third model, the unit based approach, is based on themes chosen by the teacher, ideally in cooperation with and in response to the children and their interests. Activities are planned to develop and carry out a specific theme. Units built around holidays or other special events are some of the most frequently used. The teacher helps plan the unit or theme and provides a variety of materials and resources to allow children to become involved in its development. With the unit based approach, children's literature can be used to support the chosen unit or as a base for unit plans. For example, titles with an African setting might be used for the African theme of a travel unit, or a unit based on early American life might be planned around Donald Hall's *Ox-Cart Man*. Many activities can be used as extentions of children's literature.

School-age child care programs have a variety of profiles. However, care must be given to provide a program that best meets the needs of the children who attend. Many factors influence the type program best for kindergarten through third grade children. Some of these factors include the age, abilities, and interests of the children involved; the amount of time they will be in the program; their backgrounds; and the facility and staff. Regardless of the factors, a good program should be a positive transition, before school, from home to school, and after school, from school to home. Activities for the daylong school holidays must complement both home and school.

A program with components from each model, some activities that are self-directed and others teacher-directed, both under the umbrella of a unit based plan, seem to be a natural way to meet the needs of young children and tie the parts of a good program together. A good program needs a plan based on the philosophy of the program and its goals specific to the children it serves. Responsive programming for school-age child care is supported by several factors including the total program — schedule and activities, the facility, the staff, and firsthand experiences in the community.

Schedule and Activities

For kindergarten through third grade children, one must remember that play is their work. They are beginning to engage in and seek play with a purpose, games with rules, and activities that use real materials and result in real, finished products and outcomes.

The time before school constitutes a short time when children are in child care before school begins. Activities during this time are generally self-directed. This is a quiet time within the physical limits of the facility and under the supervision of the child care staff. Children eat breakfast if provisions are made, finish homework, read, draw and color, or visit with friends. If the before school facility is not at the school, some of the time is also spent in transition from the child care facility to the school.

The time after school, although short, generally consists of three or four hours. Children need a snack, active play, group times, and choice of activity times. During school holidays and the summer, the all-day program includes periods of active play, some time for group activities, larger blocks of choice activity time, and times for snacks in the morning and afternoon, and a nutritious meal at lunchtime. After school and school holiday periods provide times for formal club meetings such as 4-H, scouts, book clubs, and special interest clubs or less formal, shorter lived clubs initiated by the children. These afternoons or longer holidays are a good time to plan for resource persons to come to the program or to take children on field trips in the community. Activities that will be extended over several days can also be planned for after school and school holidays.

Facilities and Activities

After a busy, structured day at school or during school holidays, children need opportunities for active play. An outdoor play area and/or large activity room are important. Adequate equipment for climbing and active play, and large open space for group games must be considered. Children need opportunities for physical activity both in organized indoor and outdoor play activities. Cooperative games where competition is at a minimum, but opportunities to practice and develop athletic skills, should be provided. All children need exercise and fresh air, although many will not choose serious, competitive organized games.

Each school-age child care group needs a room of its own with a place for children to keep their belongings and unfinished work. The room should have its own bulletin boards and display areas and space to set up centers for choice of activity times. The centers include a book center for reading and listening, arts and crafts, dramatic play, music, cooking, science, games, blocks and carpentry, and homework. Some programs have a television/VCR for guided viewing and a computer for special computer activities. The best room arrangement provides space for large group meetings, for quiet activities arranged away from the louder activities, and for a child to be by him/herself. Areas for small group or individual activities are best designated as centers with some permanent materials and equipment and other appropriate materials and props brought in as the theme or emphasis changes. The following discussion assumes that the school-age child care program is housed in one room. Centers may be set up in more than one room. If more than one room is used, then plans will need to be made to allow children to participate in the centers of their choice.

The book center is set up for children to have opportunity to read and enjoy books in a relaxed atmosphere. Place this center in a quiet area of the room. A bulletin board and a book rack or display area for books makes this area inviting. A cozy book corner with carpeting and pillows, bean bags, or an oversized chair makes the area relaxing. Books and appropriate magazines should be rotated on a regular basis. Some of the books available should be unit related, while others might be selected to stimulate new interests, to give children firsthand experiences with their literature classics, and to reinforce existing interests and school topics. The public library is one of the best resources for these books. Children should be encouraged to read. Some additional ways to encourage children to read is to take books outside during extended outdoor times and to devise some type of check-out system to allow children to take books home. For many children, book clubs provide a stimulus for reading.

The arts and crafts center is one of the most popular for most school-age children enjoy art activities. They need access to a variety of creative art materials and opportunities to use real tools and materials to complete craft projects. Although freedom to allow for individuality in craft projects is important, the satisfaction of a completed product as a result of following directions is also of value to school-age children. Basic art supplies to be included in the art center are scissors, glue, pencils, crayons, markers, hole punch, rulers, tape, tempera paint, and a variety of paper including wallpaper samples, paper plates, and paper bags. Collage materials such as fabric and paper scraps, trims, string, and yarn provide creative materials for children. Extra materials can then be provided for special art and craft activities.

The creative dramatics center allows children to act out their concepts of the world around them. For kindergarten and first graders, the home living area with play stove, sink, dolls, and other props as in the preschool program are appropriate. Older children enjoy a variety of other dramatic play props. Dress-up clothes and costumes make excellent creative dramatic props. Play kits with props appropriate for pretending to be a beautician, grocer, schoolteacher, or a variety of other people and characters stimulate dramatic play. A variety of kits may be made up, boxed separately, and added to the dramatic play area as needed. Parents are great resources for old uniforms and other vocation related props.

Puppets, commercial and homemade, and a puppet stage encourage creative dramatic play. The use of puppets, costumes, and other simple props in this area can be used to extend children's experiences with their literature.

The music center includes a record player and recordings and a tape player for use by the children in listening, responding to, and recording music. Simple musical instruments like an autoharp, guitar, xylophone, bells, and drums provide equipment for experimentation and practice. In a large room a piano is also desirable. A piano, autoharp, or xylophone can be color coded with the note on the instrument and the music coded with the same color. This coding method allows children to practice and learn simple tunes. Scarves make good props for creative movement. Opportunities for group singing are also important.

A *cooking center* encourages independence. Snacks may be prepared on a daily basis or on special occasions by the children. A well-supervised cooking center with equipment and ingredients for school-age children to do their own food preparation gives them firsthand experience with real life activities. Children might make shopping lists and go to the market to assist in buying ingredients for cooking experiences. Ideally, this center needs to be near a water supply and have equipment such as measuring spoons and cups, mixing bowls and spoons, a mixer, hot plate, pots and pans, electric frying pan, and a popcorn popper, to mention a few. Although children should have freedom to do their own preparations, this center does need close adult supervision.

Through the *science center*, children become more aware of their real world by participating in science experiences and observations. Plants, small animals like gerbils, or an aquarium provide live things for children to take care of. Science equipment such as magnets, scales, magnifying glasses, a thermometer, and nature displays are needed for the science center. Materials and directions for simple experiments can be available in the science center. If outdoor space is available, the planting and tending of a flower or vegetable garden provides valuable experiences for children.

A *block and construction center* provides opportunity for creative play, social interaction, and problem solving. Unit blocks with props like small trucks and cars, and plastic people and animals provide stimulus for block construction. Children often create their own props for the block area. When supervision and adequate space are available, hammers and nails, saws, and soft wood should be available for carpentry projects.

In the *game and puzzle center* a variety of materials are appropriate for school-age children. Games encourage children to practice their social skills, ability to follow directions, and competence in reading and computation. Games available might include a variety of board games, commercial and homemade, bingo, checkers, and memory games. Jigsaw puzzles are also appropriate for individual or small group activities.

Staff

The quality of the school-age child care program depends more on the staff than anything else. Good teachers know a lot about many things. They are well trained and continue to seek new ideas for working with children. They plan with individual as well as group needs and interests in mind and provide appropriate and varied materials and ideas. Children need teachers who are caring and understanding and who are sensitive and accepting of individual differences. These teachers must be good models in social relationships, coping skills, language development, and many other areas. They need to be flexible to take advantage of unplanned interests, events, and spontaneous "teachable" moments. Teachers need to be motivators who help children practice and show off their developing skills and help them feel good about themselves. Not only must these "significant others" in children's lives be accepting and sensitive, they must be optimistic and committed to helping children become independent and to begin to realize their potential in their world.

Field Trips

Field trips are one of the best ways to give children a variety of experiences in their community. These experiences help children begin to understand more about their community and their place in it. School-age children need preparation for a field trip such as what to expect, what to look for, what to do, and what safety precautions are necessary. The trip must be followed up with discussion, art activities, writing experiences, or other forms of review, summary, and evaluation. Field trips are best used as part of the unit based planning as another activity to reinforce objectives and concepts included in this approach to programming. Teachers must survey their community for resources unique to their community. Field trips can include trips to a local park, zoo, nature trail, greenhouse, farm, business, museum, historical site; municipality services such as the fire station, library, airport; and special cultural events, either actual performances or rehearsals. Parents are one of the program's best resources. Onsite visits to their places of work or having them come to the child care program are good ways to get parents involved and to give children experiences in the community.

MANAGEMENT AND GROUP SIZE

The ideal school-age group has no more than twenty-five children, with one adult for at least every ten children. Although younger children can benefit from being in a group with older children, and vice versa, it is desirable to have children grouped according to age for the majority of the time. The best arrangement seems to be to have each age grouped separately, or kindergarten through third grade in one group and older children in another. Age groupings allow for developmental needs and interests to be addressed more appropriately.

Generally, large group activities should include the whole group. This arrangement provides the opportunity for teachers and children to plan together, for everyone to hear the same announcements and plans at the same time, for children to feel more a part of the whole group, and for the group as a whole to experience teacher directed times including stories, special presentations, field trips, and group and individual sharing. Small group activities will usually include two to five children.

Many group management problems are solved if children's needs are met and if they have enough to do. It is better to have too much planned than not enough. Centers as described in this chapter are provided to give children a choice of appropriate activities. These centers ideally are in one large room. Children are given the opportunity to choose the centers they wish to participate in. Although children should be encouraged to finish one activity before they begin another, they should be allowed to move from one center to another during the choice of activity time or to find a quiet area in the room to do nothing if they choose. Most centers should be set up to accommodate one to four or five children at a time. Center time will vary with the total time available.

Teachers use good management techniques when they work from a well-developed plan with a balance of quiet and active, and teacher directed and individual choice activities. Teachers need to be well prepared, providing materials and equipment necessary to carry out activities that are unit based as well as materials that will help children use their own ideas and initiative to become involved. They have better control when materials are available and children understand what they are to do when they first begin an activity. Flexibility and sensitivity to children's interests and needs, and to unplanned teaching/learning experiences are also important. Some of the most enjoyable activities are unplanned by a spontaneous happening or idea.

RATIONALE FOR CHILDREN'S LITERATURE BASED PROGRAMMING

Responsive programming for school-age child care can certainly be supported by the use of children's literature and the many activities that can be provided to extend children's experience with this literature. One of the best ways to support the unit based approach to programming is to use children's literature either to support the unit subject or as an actual springboard for the unit.

What better way to bring children and books together than to purposefully integrate literature into the activities of the program? Children experience their literature as they read and look at books and as they hear poetry read and stories told. They learn more about books as they have opportunities to interpret them in ways that are meaningful to them. Books provide children with pleasure and enjoyment as well as resources for new ideas, information and facts, recipes, and directions for projects. Books, magazines, and other forms of literature should be made available for children to read and to go back to as often as they wish.

The purpose of this guide is to provide children's literature related programming ideas for kindergarten through third grade children, specifically in child care programs. The plan is twofold, to get children and books together and to provide ideas for large and small group or individual activities. Programming ideas are presented specifically in the area of arts and crafts, dramatic play, music, cooking, and celebrations.

In each chapter, selected children's literature titles are presented. Each title is followed by a brief annotation and activity suggestions to extend children's experiences with the title. The literature and accompanying activity may be used independently or the title and/or titles and several activities may be used together to develop a theme. Programming and theme planning notes are included where needed. Activities are suggested for individual children, small groups of children (four to six at a time), and the large group (entire group). To designate group size for which the activities are most appropriate, the following codes are used:

Individual—I

Small Group—SG

Large Group—LG

The group size and time required for activities will depend upon the complexity of the activity and the interest and abilities of the children. For the art, music, and dramatic play activities, a notation is made if the activity requires more than approximately twenty minutes. For the cooking activities, about twenty minutes should be allowed for preparation time, plus the time for cooking. Ideally, in a school-age child care program, activities for individual or small groups may be done during the choice of activity time in the designated art, music, dramatic play, and cooking centers.

In the "Let's Create" chapter, some activities are suggested to duplicate the technique the illustrator used in creating the illustrations for the book. Other suggestions are a mere spin-off of the technique, text, or subject matter.

The "Let's Pretend" chapter is arranged by genre. A variety of creative dramatic activities are presented for Bible stories, fables, folk and fairy tales, nursery rhymes, and single titles that lend themselves well to creative dramatics.

"Let's Make Music" includes suggestions for actual singing of the songs of single song picture books, making instruments, and using musical interpretations and accompaniments to selected children's literature.

"Let's Cook" suggests cooking experiences mentioned in the literature or related to the literature. Cooking experiences may be planned for snack time or for a special treat.

"Let's Celebrate" suggests several holidays and special occasions for school-age children to make plans for and to celebrate. Art, creative dramatics, music, and cooking ideas as well as other activities to develop a variety of celebration themes are presented.

The values of using children's literature as a basis for such programming are numerous. Some objectives are general while others are specific to the activity areas.

GENERAL OBJECTIVES

When children experience their literature in appropriate ways and participate in activities as an extension of this literature, they will have the following opportunities:

- To recognize, enjoy, and value many kinds of good literature.

- To have a better understanding and interpretation of the literature (the plot, characterization, and how to portray and understand feelings).

- To experience activities for an extension and sheer enjoyment of the literature.

- To encourage and guide creative imagination.

- To learn new concepts.

- To grow in social understanding and cooperation.

- To develop a positive self-concept and a feeling of worth and self-confidence through having satisfying individual and group experiences.

- To respond actively and appropriately to literature in a variety of ways.

- To experience and recognize a variety of styles and forms for the communication of ideas.

- To interpret their literature in ways that are familiar and real to them.

- To learn more about the authors and illustrators of their literature.

- To instill in children a desire to read and find out, to have a genuine interest in reading for pleasure and information.

The suggestions for literature related activities included in this guide are in the areas of creative art, dramatic play, music, cooking, and special celebration activities. Objectives specific to each activity area are presented as follows:

Creative Art Activities

- To help children identify some of the author/illustrators of their literature and the illustration techniques employed by each.

- To assist children in becoming familiar with a variety of media and techniques used to illustrate picture books.

- To give children opportunities to express their interpretations of literature through art media.

Creative Dramatics

- To provide opportunities to extend experiences with their literature through creative expression.

- To have creative avenues of expressing interpretations and understanding of the characters, plot, action, word, and setting of the literature.

Music Activities

- To help children become familiar with picture book versions of single songs.

- To have opportunities to express their interpretations of rhythm, mood, action, and characters through music and movement.

Cooking Experiences

- To help children identify children's literature on the subject of food.

- To give children opportunities to relate their literature to the real life activities of food preparation.

Celebrations

- To acquaint children with the vast amounts of literature on a variety of subjects including holidays.

- To give children a broader basis and a better understanding for celebrating their holidays.

- To stimulate children's imaginations and creativity in their celebrations.

USES OF THE SCHOOL-AGE PROGRAMMING GUIDE

Although written primarily for school-age child care teachers, children's librarians and classroom teachers will also find the ideas presented useful in planning literature based programs for the children with whom they work. Teachers and librarians may choose to use one title and an accompanying activity, one title and several activities, or a combination of titles and activities. Suggestions for a variety of approaches and activities are presented in this guide.

School-age child care teachers may use single ideas or a combination of several ideas to plan experiences and activities for the children in their programs. Titles may be used as a basis or support of the unit based program or used in appropriate centers to stimulate activities. Suggestions are made in this guide for both approaches. The brief time before and after school needs to be limited to short-term activities or to activities that can be easily carried over for several days. Full days and school holidays allow more time for more in-depth programming, for resource persons, and field trips. A special teacher directed time each day should include time where the teacher reads to the children in her group. Single titles, poetry, or chapter books may be chosen for this time. Quiet times are a good time for the teacher to set a good example of reading while children are engaging in reading or other quiet activities. The teacher can provide a variety of good reading materials for this time. Of course, kindergarten children will "read" the pictures while most children, first grade or older, will be able to read for themselves if they have access to materials on their reading level.

Children's librarians (school and public) can use many suggested activities in their library programming to extend the literature experiences of the children with whom they work. The resources and length of time children are in the library will determine the activities selected. The following suggestions are specifically for children's librarians:

- Suggest curriculum related literature and activities to teachers.

- Use a newsletter directed to children, parents, or teachers suggesting titles and accompanying activities.

- Have a special library day based on a given theme. Present chosen literature and allow children to choose from a variety of activities in which to participate.

- Sponsor book clubs. Invite children to hear good stories and to participate in fun activities as an extension of the literature.

- Have literature related bulletin boards and displays. Provide brochures suggesting specific title or titles and special activities.

An important part of the *classroom teacher's* task is to encourage their young students to read, to practice their reading skills, and to develop new skills. Children's literature can be integrated into the curriculum for the primary grades, not only language, but math, science, social studies, art, music, and other curriculum areas. Children's literature can be selected to support curriculum concepts. During the school day a special time to read books and to discuss and respond to these experiences is valuable. Single titles may be read by the teacher, or chapter books (books that can be read over a period of several days) as suggested by Trelease in his *Read-Aloud Handbook* can be used to encourage children to read.

Selection tools such as *Children's Catalog, Elementary School Library Collection,* and the index, *A to Zoo: Subject Access to Children's Picture Books*, were used to select titles for recommendation in this guide. These tools, found in most school and public libraries, may be used to identify additional or substitute titles of children's literature to use in unit/theme planning.

Before activities are begun, the literature should be presented to children in an appropriate manner. For kindergarten and first grade children, a good approach is to present the literature in a large group setting. Older children, seven- and eight-year-olds, may wish to read the book themselves before beginning the activity.

Teachers are encouraged to provide a variety of techniques and models for sharing and experiencing literature. Titles are often available in audiovisual format that may add variety to the presentation. Teachers should consult the public or school library for available titles in 16 millimeter and video formats. The *Elementary School Library Collection* is a good reference resource for identifying titles in picture book format as well as sound filmstrip, film, and recording formats.

UNIT PLANNING

A plan for an ongoing school-age child care program is important. A smooth-running, well-balanced program for school-age children is usually a result of long- and short-term planning. Each day needs a plan. Unit or theme planning helps tie many or all of these activities together and is appropriate for program planning.

Children enjoy participating in the planning process. The interest assessment part of this chapter gives ideas of how to assess children's interests and to include them in planning their activities.

Long-term planning includes unit topics for the entire school year or the summer months. Holiday/seasonal themes provide a good beginning and additional units may be added. Long-term planning allows time to arrange for field trips, special resource persons, and provisions for special materials needed. Short-term planning relates specifically to detailed planning for each unit. Units may be short, completed in one day or session, or may last for several weeks or sessions. Unit plans need to include a title (what the unit is about), subtitles or themes, purpose (a statement of the objective of the unit), book or books to be used, activities, resources, and methods of evaluating the unit. Figure 1.2 may be helpful in developing unit plans for school-age child care.

The most effective unit/theme planning includes as many related activities as possible. Theme related concepts and ideas are reinforced as related ideas for art, dramatic play, music, cooking, games, science, field trips, and special guests are used for school-age child care. The best unit planning employs the following guidelines:

- Break units down into narrow themes. Choose an object, idea, or narrow concept for a starting point to expand into a theme. For example, a unit on "signs of fall" may be broken down to themes like apples, fall colors, and the county fair.

- Have children contribute ideas of ways to investigate and develop the theme.

- Be sure to use as many of the ideas as possible shared by the children.

- Allow for discussion, sharing, and discovery about the theme topics.

- Extend the theme only as long as children are interested.

- Provide ample time to introduce the theme and related activities.

- Plan a time to share new knowledge, activities, and finished projects or products with the entire group.

- Allow children to help evaluate the unit, themes, and activities.

Programming notes throughout the activity chapters suggest ideas for theme planning. A variety of activities may be used for some themes while activities for others are more limited. To provide effective literature based programming, teachers and librarians should use the following guidelines:

- Be very familiar with the book or other type of literature to be used (know the literature or story and about the author/illustrator).

- Adapt the activities to meet the specific needs, interest, and abilities of the children in the program.

- Plan most activities for small groups of children after the literature has been presented.

- Give all children who wish to participate in a given activity or center opportunity to do so, possibly on a rotating basis.

Unit Plan Sheet

Unit:

Theme:

Objectives:

Book(s):

Bulletin Board and Displays:

Large Group Activities:

Special Activities (Individual or small group—art, drama, music, cooking, games, etc.):

Special Resources (films, people, field trips):

Active Play (outdoors/indoors):

Snacks:

Evaluation:

Fig. 1.2.

Children's literature based activities can be lots of fun, bring children and books closer together, and provide many appropriate activities and experiences for children in school-age child care.

NOTES

[1] Erik H. Erikson, *Childhood and Society*, 2nd ed. (New York: Norton, 1963), 255-61.

[2] Joan Bergstrom, *School's Out — Now What?* (Berkeley, Calif.: Ten Speed, 1984), 8.

[3] Richard T. Schofield and Jean Watson Shaw, "Programming for School-Age Children in Child Care," *Day Care and Early Education* 8 (Spring 1981): 19.

2
LET'S CREATE
Children's Literature and Creative Art Activities

Most children love art activities. They express their feelings and interpretations of the world around them through their art long before they can express themselves with written words. Literature related art activities give children opportunities to respond to their literature in creative ways. Also, children become better acquainted with author/illustrators and the variety of media and techniques they use to illustrate their picture books.

Activities are suggested in this chapter that duplicate the illustration techniques of the picture book illustrators or that extend the child's experience with the subject matter of the literature through a related activity. The illustrations become more meaningful to children as they experience for themselves the process used by the illustrator. Likewise, the subject matter of the text or illustrations becomes more real as children experience follow-up activities related to the picture book they have experienced.

Art activities in this chapter are suggested to allow children to be creative, to use their imaginations. Some of the activities are also in the craft category. Crafts are very appropriate for school-age children as they provide opportunities to use real tools, follow specific directions, and demand a definite finished product. Although a specific finished product is the end result of a craft activity, room for a personal touch or individuality is allowed.

Art activities are suggested under the assumption that basic art materials and tools such as glue, scissors, staples and stapler, yarn or string, and paint brushes are available. Special materials needed for each activity are included in the activity directions. An effort is made to suggest alternate materials when possible. The reader is encouraged to adapt the ideas when necessary.

VALUES OF USING LITERATURE BASED CREATIVE ART ACTIVITIES

- To provide for an extension of the sheer enjoyment of the literature.

- To encourage and guide creative imagination.

- To contribute to the development of a positive self-concept or feeling of worth and self-confidence through contribution in a satisfying individual or group experience.

- To learn art concepts of color, texture, line, design, movement, and direction.

- To help children with self-expression of transferring mental "pictures" or ideas into visible art creations.

- To help children develop their own sense of what is beautiful.

TECHNIQUES FOR CREATIVE ART ACTIVITIES

- Select picture books with easily recognizable illustration techniques and media types.

- Select poems or other literature that might be interpreted through an art medium.

- Present the picture book, poem, or other literature in an appropriate way (read aloud, storytelling, filmstrip, movie, recording).

- Discuss illustrations or possible illustrations.

- Discuss and demonstrate, if necessary, techniques used.

- Provide art materials for individual or group art projects.

- Allow children to be creative and to experiment with the media.

- Do not provide patterns for creative activities. Reserve patterns for craft activities.

- Plan art activities for individual expression or combine activities for a small group or class project.

- Plan to use a variety of art techniques including applying, modeling (constructing), and interlacing (weaving).

- Place books in reading or book area for children to view over and over again.

- Have basic materials available for children to use when they need them. Basics should include paper, crayons, pencils, markers, tape, glue, staples/stapler, scissors, and ruler.

METHODS OF EVALUATION

- Observe for an increased request and circulation of books, stories, authors, and illustrators used.

- Observe children's interest, participation, and requests for repeated or similar activities.

- Assess children's knowledge of authors, illustrators, and their works, through games, verbal quizzes, and other activities after they have participated in several teacher directed activities.

- Have children select a book, identify a technique, and use the same technique in their own way in an art activity.

CHILDREN'S LITERATURE AND ART ACTIVITIES

Anderson, Joan. **Pioneer Children of Appalachia.** Photographs by George Ancona. Clarion, 1986.
    Photographs from Fort New Salem, a living history museum in West Virginia, recreate the pioneer life of young people in Appalachia in the early nineteenth century. The children help with the work and crafts.

18 / LET'S CREATE

Pioneer crafts. Consult craft books to find directions for some of the crafts mentioned in this title. Have a choice of crafts for children to do. Some of the crafts photographed include cornhusk dolls, cornhusk fiddles, quilting, candle-making, and basket-weaving. (I,SG)

Craft show. Visit a craft show. Have children identify crafts they would like to try. (SG,LG)

Bangs, Edward. **Steven Kellogg's Yankee Doodle.** Illustrated by Steven Kellogg. Parent's Magazine Press, 1976.

The traditional Yankee Doodle song illustrated in picture book form.

Yankee Doodle hats. Have available newspaper and real or construction paper feather. Make a hat by folding a double thickness of newspaper as follows:

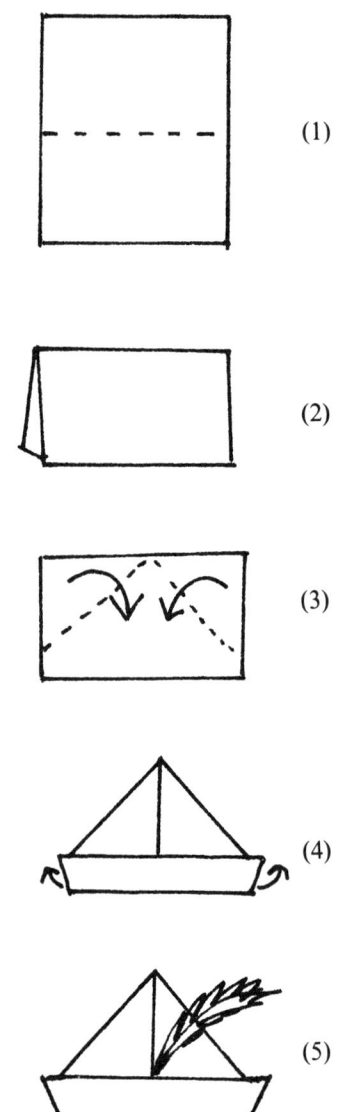

Staple if necessary. Add a real or construction paper feather. (I,SG,LG)

Programming notes: Use activity as part of an Independence Day celebration or to accompany a parade and the singing of "Yankee Doodle."

Brown, Marcia. **Stone Soup.** Scribner, 1947. Caldecott Honor Book.

An old tale of three hungry soldiers who tricked weary peasants into giving them the things they needed for soup after they threatened to make soup from stones. The soldiers were also given beds in the best homes.

Stone critters. Have available smooth stones and tempera or acrylic paints. Select smooth stones to make stone animals or critters. Paint features on the stones. Glue stones together before painting, if desired. Hint: Use chenille stems, pipe cleaners, or twigs for features. Use the small craft eyes. (I,SG)

Carle, Eric. **The Very Busy Spider.** Philomel, 1984.

The spider in the story cannot be diverted from spinning her web, although the farm animals try to do so. She shows that her web is not only beautiful but useful, as she catches the fly in her web. The fly has appeared on each page during the story. The illustrations are beautiful, vibrant collages. The spider web is actually raised from the page.

Spider web. Use glue, powdered tempera, and construction paper. Mix yellow or brown powdered tempera in glue to give it color. Apply lines of colored glue to black construction paper to make a spider web design. Allow to dry. The results will be very similar to the raised spider web designs in the illustrations of Carle's book. (I,SG)

Spider web. Provide a round cake pan, black construction paper, white tempera and a marble. Cut a circle of black construction paper to match the size of a round cake pan. Place paper in the bottom of the pan. Put a blot of white paint in the middle of the circle. Roll a marble around in the paint. Trails of white are left across the paper resembling a somewhat imperfect but fun spider web.[1] (I,SG)

Spider web. Use a styrofoam meat tray, black yarn, and plastic needles. With a plastic needle and yarn, sew in and out making a spider web design. Begin in the middle of the tray and branch out. Try to keep the design resembling a spider web. Each web will be different. (I,SG)

Spiders. Materials needed include black construction paper, yellow crayon, and rubber bands. Cut a circle from black construction paper. Cut eight strips for legs. Attach four to each side. Fold each leg in accordian style and release. Draw eyes with yellow crayon. Suspend with a cut rubber band stapled to the middle. (I,SG,LG)

Additional spider titles:

Graham, Margaret. *Be Nice to Spiders.* Harper & Row, 1967.

Kraus, Robert. *The Trouble with Spiders.* Harper & Row, 1962.

McDermott, Gerald. *Anansi the Spider.* Holt, Rinehart and Winston, 1972. Caldecott Honor Book.

White, E. B. *Charlotte's Web.* Illustrated by Garth Williams. Harper & Row, 1952.

Programming notes: A theme on spiders can easily be developed using the titles and activities presented here. Look for informational sources and pictures for children to study. They will like the realistic information. The spider theme can be used as part of the Halloween unit. The theme can be completed in one program session in the library or be extended for two or three days in a child care setting. For the child care setting, E. B. White's *Charlotte's Web* can be used as a read-aloud story; read a chapter a day at quiet time.

Cendrars, Blaise. **Shadow.** Translated and illustrated by Marcia Brown. Scribner, 1982. Caldecott Medal Award.

African folk tale style illustrated with collage and paints. Shadow is illustrated as solid black throughout the book. The story is the illustrator's own translation and illustration of the French poem, "The Sorcerer."

Solographics. Have available sun-sensitive paper or dark construction paper and leaf or other objects or shapes of choice. Place an object with an interesting shape on sun-sensitive paper.

Place paper with object on it in the sunlight. Wait a few minutes, then develop sun-sensitive paper in tap water. Or use plain dark construction paper and leave in the sun for at least one day. Either way a unique print is made by the sun. Note: Sun-sensitive paper is rather expensive and sometimes hard to find. School supply and craft supply companies are the best sources. (I,SG)

Silhouettes. Have available large (at least 12 by 18 inches) pieces of black and white construction paper for each child, a gooseneck lamp or filmstrip projector, and white chalk. Tape a black piece of paper to a wall. Have child sit sideways in a chair near the paper. Turn on a bright light, either a gooseneck lamp or a filmstrip projector lamp. Trace around the shadow profile on the black paper with a pencil or white chalk. Cut silhouette out and glue it on white construction paper. Repeat for each child who wishes a silhouette. Hint: Use light paper for silhouette and mount on dark paper. Silhouettes make great Valentine, Mother's Day, or Grandparents' Day presents. (I,SG)

Silhouettes. Have available flat forms or shapes, a variety of construction paper, and if desired each child can make a background picture drawn with colored chalk or painted with tempera. Trace around desired forms or make your own shapes on dark construction paper. Cut out and glue shapes on lighter construction paper or the drawn background picture similar to illustrations in *Shadows*. (I,SG,LG)

Additional shadow titles:

De Regniers, Beatrice S. *The Shadow Book.* Illustrated by Isabel Gordon. Harcourt, Brace, Jovanovich, 1960.

Mahy, Margaret. *The Boy with Two Shadows.* Illustrated by Jenny Williams. Watts, 1971.

Programming notes: To develop a theme on shadows, use the titles and activities listed here plus suggestions for celebrating Groundhog Day in the "Let's Celebrate" chapter. Groundhog Day is a very appropriate time to use the shadows theme.

Cooney, Barbara. **Chanticleer and the Fox.** Crowell, 1958. Caldecott Medal Award.
Story is that adapted from Geoffrey Chaucer's *Chanticleer and the Fox.* Chanticleer, the rooster, outsmarts the fox to get away from him. Illustrations use the scratch board technique.
Scratch board. Have available crayons, drawing paper, and toothpicks or blunt scissors. Crayon lightly on background paper. Use one or several colors. Color over the background colors heavily with black crayon. Use toothpick or blunt scissors to scratch out a design. Note: This art activity uses a method most children have not experienced but will enjoy. (I,SG,LG)

De Paola, Tomie. **Andy: That's My Name.** Prentice-Hall, 1973.
Andy has fun with the letters of his name. He cannot read but the older children make other words with letters of his name.
Name collage. Collect newspapers and magazines for this activity. Have each child make a collage of letters in his name. Find and cut out letters of name. Arrange and glue on a piece of construction paper as desired. Continue the activity until the whole page is covered with repeated arrangements of his name. (I,SG,LG)
Name collage. Have on hand poster board and magazines. Print name in large connected block letters on poster board. Have each child find pictures to cut and glue on letters that relate to interests, likes and dislikes, and favorite things. Each child's name will be unique because of the individual differences illustrated. (I)
Name game. This activity requires only paper and pencil, some spelling skills, and/or a dictionary. Write name on the center top of the page. Have child write down as many words as he can using only the letters of his name. (I)
Acrostic. Have paper and pencil available. Try an acrostic. Write name vertically. Find words that fit in the acrostic with letters of the name. (I,SG,LG). For example:

```
    Ant                         Mom
    paN                         Arm
    Dad                         Run
    toY                         Yes
```

Programming notes: Children love to see their names in print. Use this title and activities at the beginning of the year for a get acquainted activity.

De Paola, Tomie. **The Popcorn Book.** Holiday House, 1978.

A story about popcorn based on factual information of how it is grown, harvested, stored, and cooked. Colorful, humorous illustrations.

Popcorn pictures. Have available popped corn, construction paper, crayons, and glue. Use popped corn to represent blossoms or snow for spring or winter scenes. Make tree trunk by drawing with crayons or using construction paper for back. Draw or glue trunk on a large piece of construction paper. Place dots of glue where popcorn is to be placed. Place popcorn in glue. Allow to dry before removing from a flat surface. (I,SG)

Popcorn mosaic. Have colored popcorn kernels, tagboard, and glue available. Use popcorn kernels to make a seed collage or mosaic. Colored kernels work well for the mosaic. Brush slightly diluted glue on the area each color of corn is to be placed. Use tagboard or other heavy type paper. Allow to dry on a flat surface. (I,SG)

Programming notes: This title may be used to support the American Indian theme. Or merely present the title in large group, followed by popping corn for snack and art activities.

Emberley, Barbara. **One Wide River to Cross.** Illustrated by Ed Emberley. Prentice-Hall, 1966. Caldecott Honor Book.

A picture book interpretation of an old folk song about the animals going into Noah's Ark. Illustrations are woodcuts using black against brightly colored backgrounds.

Potato printing. Have available a potato, knife, tempera paint, and art paper. Carve a design on a potato cut in half. Cut away part of potato around design that is not to be part of the print. Dip potato with design in tempera paint. Select dark colors for light paper or light colors for dark paper. Print on paper as many times as desired. (I,SG)

Model clay printing. Secure modeling clay, toothpicks or nail, tempera paint, and paper. Form design from clay. Make lines in design with a nail or toothpick. Use the printing process as described in potato printing. (I,SG)

Cookie cutter printing. Select cookie cutters with desired design. Use the printing process as described for potato printing. (I,SG)

Styrofoam cut. Provide styrofoam meat packing trays, primary pencil, tempera paint with a small amount of liquid detergent, and newsprint. Use a styrofoam meat packing tray with the sides trimmed off. Draw design on the piece of styrofoam. Make a good impression with a primary pencil. Coat the entire area including the design with paint. Cover with a piece of newsprint, rub, and lift. Design will transfer. Hints: Experiment to get the appropriate amount of paint on the styrofoam for the desired transfer. Remember, if letters or words are printed, they must be backwards to transfer correctly. A small amount of liquid detergent mixed with tempera helps it adhere. (I,SG)

Additional woodcut titles:

Brown, Marcia. *Once a Mouse.* Scribner, 1961. Caldecott Medal Award.

Emberley, Barbara. *Drummer Hoff.* Illustrated by Ed Emberley. Prentice-Hall, 1967. Caldecott Medal Award.

Gag, Wanda. *Millions of Cats.* Coward, McCann, and Geoghegan, 1928.

22 / LET'S CREATE

Programming notes: Woodcuts are unique ways children's books are illustrated. Use the titles to show this method and follow up with art activities. Have actual woodcuts available if possible. Find a local artist who uses the woodcut technique. Have him display his art and demonstrate his techniques. Allow children to experiment with more than one way to do simulated woodcuts. This technique makes good Christmas, Valentine, and other greeting cards and decorative wrapping paper.

Ets, Marie Hall. **Gilberto and the Wind.** Viking, 1963.

A story of a Mexican boy and his struggle to fly a kite because of his unpredictable friend, the wind.

Kite. Use a paper plate, streamers, and string to make a kite. Make a very simple kite by attaching a string to one side. Punch a hole in the side of the plate to thread the string through before tying. Attach streamers of lightweight material or crepe paper to the other side. Decorate the plate if desired. (I,SG,LG)

Programming notes: Use this title during the spring or other windy times of the year. After making kites be sure to allow time to try them out.

Ets, Marie Hall. **Nine Days to Christmas.** Viking, 1959. Caldecott Medal Award.

A story of a Mexican Christmas and the search for the right piñata! The pictures capture the preparation and celebration of the Christmas season as five-year-old Ceci plans her own posada, parties held on the nine days before Christmas.

Piñata. Have available a grocery bag, newspaper, wrapped candies, yarn, streamers, and paints or felt tipped markers. Stuff a paper bag with newspapers and candies. Tie at the top. Decorate with streamers, paints, or whatever you desire. Hang with a sturdy string. Take turns hitting the piñata with a stick until it breaks. Enjoy the treats. This can be a group project. Note: This is a very simple piñata. Make one as fancy as you wish. Have a small group of children make the piñata for the large group to use or divide the group into several small groups and have each group make their own piñata. Use this activity at Christmas time. (SG,LG)

Freeman, Don. **A Rainbow of My Own.** Viking, 1966.

A little boy tries to capture a rainbow. It disappears so he invents one of his own. Beautifully illustrated book about rainbows. Colored pencils and watercolors are used for illustrations.

A rainbow of my own. Use colored pencils, watercolors, and drawing paper. Make a rainbow with colored pencils. Use watercolors to complete the picture in the fashion of the illustration by Freeman. Note: Experiment a little with pencils and watercolors and the combination before making the picture. (I,SG)

Additional rainbow titles:

Carle, Eric. *Let's Paint a Rainbow.* Philomel, 1982.

Sandburg, Carl. *Rainbows Are Made: Poems by Carl Sandburg.* Selected by L. B. Hopkins. Harcourt, Brace, Jovanovich, 1982.

Wood, Audrey. *The Napping House.* Illustrated by Don Wood. Harcourt, Brace, Jovanovich, 1984.

Programming notes: Plan a springtime unit. Use the rainbow titles plus Marie Hall Ets's *Gilberto and the Wind,* Gene Zion's *Really Spring,* and poems about spring from such collections as *In a Spring Garden* and *The Random House Book of Poetry for Children.* Use one session for each of the following springtime themes: the wind, signs of spring, rainbows, and animal life in the spring.

Ginsburg, Mirra. **Ookie-Spooky.** Illustrated by Emily McCully. Crown Publishers, 1979.

Masha draws many familiar things in her new book but also something quite unusual, a spooky monster from her imagination. Many of the illustrations are a child's line drawing done with crayons or colored chalk.

Crayon drawings. Use crayons or colored chalk on drawing paper. Have pupils draw their own "Ookie-Spooky" with crayons or colored chalk. Encourage children to use their imagination. Share with the entire group or display on the bulletin board. Note: If colored chalk is used, spray finished picture with nonaerosol hair spray or brush the paper with diluted evaporated milk before drawing. Both serve as a fixative. (I,SG)

Ghost or secret pictures. Have available a candle or paraffin, slick drawing paper, and diluted dark tempera. Draw with a candle or paraffin on paper. Paint over the entire piece of paper with diluted tempera. Black or blue works well. (I,SG)

Ookie goop. Make ookie goop. This medium provides an unusual material to play with. Does not get to a moldable consistency. The fun is in the feeling and playing. Caution: Do not put on paper or cloth. It sticks like glue.

Ookie Goop

1/3 cup Elmer's Glue
1/4 cup liquid laundry starch

Mix with your hands until you can pick it up. Add starch to make it thicken.
(I,SG)

Programming notes: Use this title and activities and Maurice Sendak's *Where the Wild Things Are* as part of a Halloween unit. Monsters can be the theme. Encourage children to use their imaginations as they create their own monsters.

Hall, Donald. **Ox-Cart Man.** Illustrated by Barbara Cooney. Viking, 1979. Caldecott Medal Award.

An early American New England farmer travels by ox-cart, sells his family's products, and returns home to make more goods. Colorful folk art style illustrations done with acrylics.

Watercolors or tempera. Provide a variety of vivid colored tempera paints and art paper. Paint an early American scene. Use vivid colors as in *Ox-Cart Man*. Seasonal pictures may be painted. (I,SG)

Log cabins. Provide one-half pint or pint milk cartons, brown tempera with liquid detergent, materials for logs, construction paper, and glue. Paint a one-half pint or pint milk carton with brown tempera with a small amount of liquid detergent added. Glue on a choice of materials for logs (pretzels, small twigs, matchsticks, toothpicks, or construction paper) on all sides of the carton. Make windows, doors, and roof from construction paper and glue on carton.[2] (SG)

Simulated quilting (patchwork). Have available quilt designs and patterns, wallpaper samples, construction paper, and tracing paper. Decide on quilt design. Trace pattern and cut out pieces from wallpaper samples. Arrange pieces to make the design and glue on a large piece of paper. Display different designs and color and pattern combinations. (I,SG)

Other early American crafts. Consult craft books found in craft shops or the public library for direction and other crafts such as stenciling, quilting (for potholders, pillow covers, or tote bags), candle-making, candle-wicking, embroidery, or cross-stitching. (I,SG,LG)

Programming notes: An extensive early American theme can easily be developed using this title. For an afternoon or short library program, either one of the less complicated activities should be chosen or several related activities should be provided from which children may choose. In the child care setting, several days may be spent on this theme using arts and crafts, cooking activities, games, and music appropriate to the time to provide a variety of theme related activities.

Hoban, Tana. **Circles, Triangles, and Squares.** Macmillan, 1974.

A book of shapes. Photographs of things in a child's world that are circles, triangles, and squares.

Shape book. Provide construction paper, typing paper, and magazines. Fold paper in half. Decorate the outside of folded construction paper for the cover. Use the typing paper for inside pages. Make your own shape book. Cut and paste pictures of chosen shapes from magazines or catalogs. Make separate pages for each shape. Staple pages together on the fold. (I,SG)

Shape posters. Have available poster board, magazines, and catalogs. Cut poster board in shape of circle, triangle, or square. Draw or cut and paste pictures of things that are the same shape. Display posters. Note: School-age children could make shape books or posters for preschoolers to use. (I,SG)

Examine Hoban's books. Have children examine all of Tana Hoban's books and decide on their own activities as an extension of each book.

Additional Hoban titles:

Hoban, Tana. *I Read Signs.* Greenwillow, 1983.

_____ . *I Read Symbols.* Greenwillow, 1983.

_____ . *Round and Round and Round.* Greenwillow, 1983.

_____ . *Shapes, Shapes, Shapes.* Greenwillow, 1986.

Hoban, Tana. **Is It Red? Is It Yellow? Is It Blue?** Greenwillow, 1978.

A book of colors. Each page contains colored photographs matched in bold rounds of color at the bottom of each page. The familiar objects photographed are very appealing to children and help them identify the colors red, yellow, blue, orange, green, and purple.

Color book. Have available construction paper, typing paper, crayons or colored markers, magazines, and catalogs. Put book together as suggested for shape book. Allow children to choose how they will illustrate their book about colors. They may cut and paste pictures from magazines or catalogs for colors chosen, or with crayons make their own pictures to depict chosen colors. Encourage them to illustrate only one color per page. Note: A great idea would be for school-age children to make color books for preschoolers. Laminate each page and put them together to make a book. (I,SG)

Programming notes: Hoban uses another form of illustration, that of photography. Children may duplicate this technique by finding magazine and other pictures to cut and paste to illustrate their own books. For older children, initiate a photography club; they might enjoy illustrating their own book with photographs.

Hutchins, Pat. **Rosie's Walk.** Macmillan, 1968.

A wordless book about a hen escaping from a fox in the barnyard. Excellent illustrations that clearly convey the fact that the hen is not aware that the fox is after her.

Barnyard map. Provide large sheets of paper or poster board, crayons or markers, and a local map. Talk about maps. Look at simple maps of your community, if available. Check with the local chamber of commerce. Using crayons or markers, draw a picture of Rosie's walk around the barnyard. Expand the idea by encouraging the child to draw a map of his immediate community. Hint: Encourage child to make a small sketch of the map he wishes to draw and then transfer his ideas to the larger paper. This allows him to change his mind and to try different ideas. (I,SG)

Johnson, Crockett. **Harold and the Purple Crayon.** Harper & Row, 1955.
    Harold used his purple crayon to take an imaginary trip. He draws roads, boats, and a balloon to help him. He encounters a terrible dragon, but is able to escape with the aid of his crayon. Illustrations are in black and white except for his purple drawings.
    Crayon drawings. Have crayons and paper available. Encourage children to select their favorite color to draw a picture using their imaginations to make up their own story. Label each picture "(child's name) and the (chosen color) crayon."

    Programming notes: Use this title and activity in the art center or as an example of several picture book illustration techniques. Arrange children's drawings for a bulletin board display. (I,SG,LG)

Keats, Ezra Jack. **Dreams.** Macmillan, 1974.
    Amy dreams that the mouse Robert made at school saves Archie's cat from a dog. Illustrations use the collage technique with the sky scenes being marbleized paper.
    Marbleizing. Provide disposable aluminum rectangular cake pans, water, oil based or acrylic paint, and art paper. Fill disposable aluminum rectangular cake pans with water. Drop oil based or acrylic paint onto the water. Stir slightly with a stick to make interesting patterns. Place a piece of paper face down in the water and gently lift it up. Let paper dry thoroughly. Use as a picture or as desired.[3] (SG)

    Additional marbleizing titles:

Keats, Ezra Jack. *Jenny's Hat.* Harper & Row, 1966.

Lewis, Richard, ed. *In a Spring Garden.* Illustrated by Ezra Jack Keats. Dial, 1965.

Keats, Ezra Jack. **Regards to the Man in the Moon.** Four Winds, 1981.
    Louie and his friends build a spaceship from items in his father's junkyard. Louie's parents convinced him that junk is useful, not something to be ashamed of.
    Spaceships. Have children help plan and contribute materials needed to make small spaceship models. School-age children love to construct and make three-dimensional creations. Have a box of "junk" (boxes, bottle caps, material, and paper scraps), glue, scissors and other material for spontaneous creativity. Display creations. (I,SG)

Keats, Ezra Jack. **The Snowy Day.** Viking, 1962. Caldecott Medal Award.
    This book sparkles with atmosphere as it relates the joy experienced by a small boy on a snowy day. Illustrations are colorful collage and paints.
    Collage. Have a variety of collage materials available. Make a snowy day picture using cotton, construction paper, fabric scraps, and wallpaper. Glue materials on poster board or tagboard. (I,SG)
    Snowy picture. Provide cotton swabs (Q-tips®) or sponge piece attached to a clothespin, white tempera paint, and dark construction paper. Dip a cotton swab or sponge piece in white paint. Apply as desired to dark paper to make a snowy day picture. A stamping or up and down motion for application works best. Note: Cotton swabs will make smaller, more uniform snowflakes. Painting with sponges covers a larger area and provides a more varied application. (I,SG)
    Snowflakes. Provide thin white paper and good scissors. Cut a circle from thin white paper. Fold the circle in half and then into thirds. Fold third in half again.

26 / LET'S CREATE

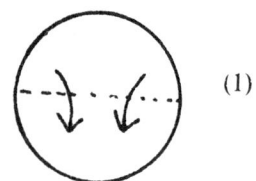 (1)

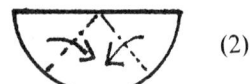 (2)

 (3)

Cut notches out of folded edges and around curve. Open. Each snowflake should be different. Part of the fun is the surprise in the design when the snowflake is opened out. (I,SG,LG)

Keats, Ezra Jack. **The Trip.** Greenwillow, 1978.
    Louie is very lonely when his family moves until he builds a shoe box diorama and goes back through it to his old neighborhood. His old friends are dressed in frightening Halloween costumes. After a visit he returns to his new neighborhood to celebrate Halloween with his new friends.
    Shoe box diorama. Provide shoe boxes, construction paper, other collage materials, and modeling clay. Allow children to collect small rocks and twigs and other nature items they might use. In the fashion of Louie's shoe box model, encourage children to make a model of their neighborhood, a room in their house, or their yard or school area. School-age children love to make three-dimensional objects. (I,SG)

    Programming notes: School-age children enjoy knowing more about the author/illustrators of their literature. There are several ways this can be accomplished.

- Compare the works of author/illustrators that use the same illustration techniques such as collage, gouache, watercolor, woodcut, photography, or pen and ink. For example: One of Keats' primary illustration techniques is collage. Compare his illustrations with those of Eric Carle, Leo Lionni, and other illustrators that use collage. Have children experiment with collage materials unique to each illustrator.

- Learn information about selected author/illustrators. Where they live, what their interests are, and why they like to illustrate children's books.

- Select a different author/illustrator to highlight each month.
  —Find out about him.
  —Display or use in some way as many of his titles as are available.
  —Use not only book format but present the literature in other available formats such as films, filmstrips, and videos.

Lionni, Leo. **A Color of His Own.** Pantheon Books, 1975.

Different colors are presented through a chameleon who is distressed about having no color of his own. As characteristic of chameleons, this chameleon changes colors as his surroundings change.

Collage. Have each child choose his/her favorite color and find pictures, paper, fabric scraps, wallpaper samples, paints, and other things to make a "color of his own" picture or poster. What is your favorite color? (I,SG)

Additional title:

Carle, Eric. *The Mixed-Up Chameleon.* New ed. Crowell, 1984.

Lionni, Leo. **Frederick.** Pantheon Books, 1967.

A creative story about how a field mouse gets ready for winter. Collage illustrations use torn paper, cut paper, and patterned wallpaper.

Collage. Provide construction paper and patterned wallpaper. Make your own collage cutting and/or tearing construction paper and cutting patterned wallpaper in desired shapes. Glue to desired size of paper to make collage picture. The collage need not be monochromatic. Use a variety of colors. (I,SG)

Additional titles:

_____ . *What?* Pantheon Books, 1983.

_____ . *When?* Pantheon Books, 1983.

_____ . *Where?* Pantheon Books, 1983.

_____ . *Who?* Pantheon Books, 1983.

Wordless board books using the same field mouse characters and collage technique illustrations.

Lionni, Leo. **Let's Make Rabbits.** Pantheon Books, 1982.

A delightful story of two rabbits—a pencil rabbit and a scissors rabbit—and their activities. Illustrations are given for both rabbits: the pencil rabbit is drawn with a pencil and the scissors rabbit is cut from wallpaper samples.

Rabbits. Have paper, wallpaper samples, pencil, scissors, and glue available. Carefully look at illustrations. Draw a rabbit with a pencil. Then with wallpaper samples make a scissors rabbit collage style. (I,SG)

Programming notes: Use this title with the spring or Easter theme. See additional suggestions in the "Let's Celebrate" chapter. School-age children enjoy this technique for making rabbits. Display creations for everyone to see.

Lionni, Leo. **Little Yellow, Little Blue.** Astor-Honor, 1959.

Story of yellow and blue and what happens when they are joined together. Collage illustrations show that green is the result of combining blue and yellow.

Collage. Provide blue and yellow tissue paper, diluted glue or evaporated milk, a brush, and background paper. Cut or tear blue and yellow tissue paper in any shape you wish. Brush diluted glue or evaporated milk on paper. Place tissue paper on glue, overlapping some of the blue and yellow. For a better mixture of colors wet the top of the tissue paper with the glue or milk. What happens? Repeat several times. (I,SG)

Blot painting. Prepare blue and yellow tempera paint. Have white or manila paper. Fold 8½-by-11-inch piece of white or manila paper in half. Open paper and drop small amounts of paint (several drops of each color) near the center of the paper. Close and rub. Open. What happens? (I,SG)

Color mix. Have blue and yellow food coloring, small bowls of water, and paper towels or coffee filters. Place several drops of blue and yellow food coloring in water in separate containers. Fold paper towel or coffee filter several times. Dip two corners in yellow and two in blue. Squeeze out excess water. Open. What happens? (I,SG)

Programming notes: Use *Little Yellow, Little Blue,* Peter Spier's *Oh, Were They Ever Happy*, and Don Freeman's *A Rainbow of My Own* for a unit on colors, color combinations, and watercolor techniques. Have a watercolor artist visit to describe and demonstrate water painting techniques. Visit an art class or art show where paintings are exhibited. Have your own art show. Display children's art work. (LG)

Lionni, Leo. **Swimmy.** Pantheon Books, 1963. Caldecott Honor Book.

A small fish finds himself alone in a huge and perplexing ocean until his natural leadership ability wins the respect of many. Collage illustrations of watercolor wash, ink, rubber stamp, pencil, and stencil are a delightful interpretation of sea life.

Underwater scene. Make an underwater scene using a paper plate, crayons, and diluted blue tempera paint. Draw an underwater scene (fish, seaweed, other sea life) with crayons on a paper plate. Brush with very diluted blue tempera. For display punch a hole in plate and tie on a yarn hanger. (I,SG)

Underwater scene. Use a paper plate; crayons, diluted tempera, or watercolors; paper; glue; and plastic wrap. Color a paper plate blue using crayons, diluted tempera, watercolors, or a sponge dabbed in blue paint. Glue fish and other sea life cut from construction paper or drawn and cut out on to painted plate. Cut out the center of another plate. Attach plastic wrap with glue or tape over hole. Turn plate upside down and attach to the one with the scene by stapling edges together. Look through the plastic to see the scene. (I,SG)

Fish print. Use a medium-sized fish with fairly large scales and fins (sole, salmon, or cod). Brush the fish with a water based paint or ink to cover it completely. Lay a piece of rice paper or white paper over the fish and carefully smooth it down to cover the fish completely. Rub the scales and fins carefully. Lift off the prints. Frame or mount the prints. A smelly process, but a nice finished product. (I,SG)

Underwater scene. Use a 12-by-18-inch piece of paper, diluted blue tempera, contrasting colors of tempera, and sponge. Paint entire paper with diluted blue tempera. Allow to dry. Cut from sponges shapes of fish, seaweed, starfish, and other sea life. Dip sponge in tempera and apply design to the blue painted paper. The result looks like an underwater scene. (I,SG,LG)

Additional sea life titles:

Lionni, Leo. *Fish Is Fish.* Pantheon Books, 1970.

MacDonald, Golden. *The Little Island.* Illustrated by Leonard Weisgard. Doubleday, 1946. Caldecott Medal Award.

Programming notes: Develop a sea life theme. Use the titles and activities suggested above. Consider adding some of the following activities:

- Find information books about fish. Help children identify and learn more about fish. Find out what is needed for fish to live.

- View an educational film on sea life.

- Visit an aquarium.

- Set up an aquarium for the room or library. Make plans for caring for the fish.

- Visit a fish market.

- Go fishing.

- Visit the beach, if location permits.

- Collect shells for shell crafts.

- Do sand casting.

McDermott, Gerald. **Arrow to the Sun.** Viking, 1974. Caldecott Medal Award.

A Pueblo Indian folk tale. Illustrations are bright yellow, orange, and brown graphic Indian designs.

Indian designs. Provide graph paper and thin felt tipped pens. Make designs with pens on the graph paper. Note: Designs that mirror each other are attractive, challenging, and fun to try. (I,SG)

Sand painting. Use sandpaper of varying textures, coarse to fine. Draw Indian designs lightly with pencil on sandpaper. Color in the designs with crayon, felt tipped pens, or tempera paint. (I,SG)

Sand painting. Have available sand, powdered tempera, and wooden plaques or cardboard (8 by 10 inches or smaller). Draw Indian designs lightly on wooden plaque or cardboard. Use powdered tempera to color sand. Use as many different colors as you wish. Apply glue to various sections of design (one color at a time). Sprinkle colored sand in glue area and shake off excess. Repeat for each color. (I,SG)

Indian jewelry. Use large elbow macaroni, tempera paint, and yarn. Paint large macaroni with tempera paint. Allow to dry. String on yarn and tie for necklaces. Note: For turquoise jewelry use turquoise colored tempera. Another way to color macaroni is to soak macaroni in a food coloring and water mixture, drain, and dry before stringing. (I,SG)

Indian leather. Collect large paper grocery bags for this activity. Cut open and trim grocery bags to have flat pieces of brown paper. Crumple pieces of grocery bags. Soak in water. Spread out and allow to dry. When dry the paper resembles simulated leather. Paint or draw with markers Indian designs or messages. Use Indian symbols. Edges may be torn to look more authentic. (I,SG)

Indian crafts. School-age children enjoy Indian crafts such as basket-making, pottery, weaving, and bead-making. Find a resource person to help children with chosen crafts or consult craft books in the public library to learn more about Indian crafts and how they are done. (I,SG,LG)

Additional Indian titles:

Clark, Ann Nolan. *The Little Indian Basket Maker.* Illustrated by Harrison Begay. Melmont, 1957.

_____ . *The Little Indian Pottery Maker.* Illustrated by Don Perceval. Melmont, 1955.

De Paola, Tomie. *The Legend of the Bluebonnet.* Putnam's Sons, 1983.

Friskey, Margaret. *Indian Two Feet and His Eagle Feather.* Illustrated by John Hawkinson and Lucy O. Hawkinson. Children's Press, 1967.

Goble, Paul. *The Girl Who Loved Wild Horses.* Bradbury, 1978. Caldecott Medal Award.

30 / LET'S CREATE

Longfellow, Henry Wadsworth. *Hiawatha.* Illustrated by Susan Jeffers. Dial, 1983.

Moon, Grace. *One Little Indian.* Whitman, 1967.

Programming notes: Develop an American Indian theme. Use the theme during September around the time of American Indian Day or during the Thanksgiving celebration. Suggestions for the American Indian theme are found in the "Let's Celebrate" chapter for American Indian Day.

Marzollo, Jean, comp. **The Rebus Treasury.** Illustrated by Carol Devine Carson. Dial, 1986.

A collection of over forty familiar rhymes and songs presented in rebus style where pictures are substituted for some of the words in the text. School-age children enjoy decoding the rhymes and songs and viewing the pictures.

Make a rebus. Supply paper, felt tipped markers, or pencils and crayons. Encourage children to select a familiar nursery rhyme or poem to write in rebus style. Display a rebus for others to see. After children have used familiar rhymes, they may wish to make an original rebus. (I,SG)

(I love you.)

Additional rebus title:

Hooks, William H., Joanne Oppenheim, and Betty D. Boegehold. *Read a Rebus.* Illustrated by Lynn Munsinger. Random House, 1986.

Programming notes: Use this technique to write valentine, birthday, or other special day notes.

Mosel, Arlene. **Tikki Tikki Tembo.** Illustrated by Blair Lent. Holt, Rinehart and Winston, 1968.

A Chinese folk tale that relates why the Chinese give all their children short names. Because of his long name, Tikki Tikki Tembo almost drowned when he fell in the well and it took his brother so long to say his name. The illustrations depict Chinese life and dress.

Pagoda. Have available half-gallon milk cartons and construction paper. Make a pagoda by painting a half-gallon milk carton with bright tempera mixed with a little detergent to make it adhere to the carton. Make two or three balconies from construction paper by tracing around the bottom of the milk carton and extending one or two inches. Cut the center from the balcony and slip on to carton. Make windows and doors with construction paper or felt tipped markers.[4] (I,SG)

Chinese lanterns. Save oatmeal boxes and tissue paper for this activity. Use oatmeal boxes. Cut out rectangular or square windows. Decorate with tissue paper and Chinese designs. Attach a string to the top for hanging or carrying. (I,SG)

Chinese dragon. Use a large corrugated box and a long piece of paper or fabric for this group project. Decorate a large corrugated box for the head of the dragon. Decorate with paints and/or brightly colored paper. Attach the long piece of paper or cloth to the box for the body of the dragon. The body should be at least 8 feet long. Have a parade. Children make the dragon mobile by hiding under the head and the body. Their legs become the dragon's legs. (SG)

Flags and banners. Consult encyclopedia and other resources to find out what the Chinese flag looks like. Also, find resources that depict Chinese designs and symbols. Using this information, make flags and banners using the designs and symbols and bright colors. (I,SG)

Additional titles on China:

Bishop, Claire H. *The Five Chinese Brothers.* Illustrated by Kurt Wiese. Coward, McCann, and Geoghegan, 1938.

Flack, Marjorie. *The Story of Ping.* Illustrated by Kurt Wiese. Viking, 1933.

Programming notes: Use the ideas and titles here to develop a theme on China. See suggestions in the "Let's Celebrate" chapter for the Chinese New Year celebration.

Munari, Bruno. **Bruno Munari's ABC.** Collins Publishers, 1960.
Large letters and pictures appropriate for younger children.
ABC book. Use wallpaper or construction paper for cover and thinner paper for pages. Have magazines and catalogs available. Provide a page for each letter. Draw or cut and paste letter on paper. Select pictures of things that begin with each letter of the alphabet. Glue on appropriate page. Design cover as you wish. Note: ABC books can also be made by drawing pictures to represent each letter. Make ABC books for a preschooler to have. (I,SG)

Additional ABC titles:

Anno, Mitsumasa. *Anno's Alphabet.* Crowell, 1974.

Burningham, John Mackintosh. *John Burningham's ABC.* Bobbs-Merrill, 1967.

Crews, Donald. *We Read: A to Z.* Harper & Row, 1967.

Emberley, Edward R. *Ed Emberley's ABC.* Little, Brown, & Co., 1978.

Fife, Dale. *Adam's ABC.* Little, Brown, & Co., 1971.

Fujikawa, Gyo. *Gyo Fujikawa's A to Z Picture Book.* Grosset and Dunlap, 1974.

Greenaway, Kate. *A Apple Pie.* Warner, 1886.

Lobel, Arnold. *On Market Street.* Illustrated by Anita Lobel. Greenwillow, 1981.

Oxenbury, Helen. *Helen Oxenbury's ABC of Things.* Watts, 1971.

Sendak, Maurice. *Alligators All Around.* Harper & Row, 1962.

Tudor, Tasha. *A Is for Annabelle.* Walck, 1954.

Wildsmith, Brian. *Brian Wildsmith's ABC.* Watts, 1963.

Prelutsky, Jack, selector. **The Random House Book of Poetry for Children: A Treasury of 572 Poems for Today's Child.** Selected by Jack Prelutsky. Illustrated by Arnold Lobel. Random House, 1983.
An excellent collection of children's poems indexed by author, title, first line, and *subject.*
Illustrate a poem. Use a poem such as "Spring Is" (p. 42). Read a selected poem to the children or have them read it several times. Provide paints, markers or crayons, and paper. Encourage children to illustrate the poem in their own way. Illustrations may be line for line or illustrate the

mood of the poem. If a group project, make a bulletin board. Display the poem and the illustrations. Note: Older children may write and illustrate their own poems. Younger children need to dictate their poem for the teacher to write and then make their own illustrations. Poetry writing is stimulated by providing a subject for children to write about or the first line for children to add to. Some children draw or paint a picture about a chosen subject and then write or dictate his poem. (I,SG,LG)

Programming notes: Have a special poetry emphasis. Select and read several poems. Have children choose the poem they would like to illustrate. Also, encourage children to write or dictate their own poems. Display the poems and illustrations. Many children's poem collections are available.

Rylant, Cynthia. **When I Was Young in the Mountains.** Illustrated by Diane Goode. Dutton, 1982. Caldecott Honor Book.

A young girl recalls her life in the mountains in the rural south. Beautiful illustrations accurately depict rural mountain life.

Craft show. Visit a craft show which displays handmade crafts or invite craftsmen to visit your program. Ask craftsmen to demonstrate their craft. Follow up with a craft or crafts children can do. Mountain crafts including making cornhusk dolls, wooden toys and figures, quilts, cross-stitching and other needlework, braided rugs, crocheting, and other crafts unique to the given mountain areas. Consult suggestions for Donald Hall's *Ox-Cart Man* for additional ideas. (LG)

Additional title:

Anderson, Joan. *Pioneer Children of Appalachia.* Photographs by George Ancona. Clarion, 1986.

Scheer, Julian. **Rain Makes Applesauce.** Illustrated by Marvin Bileck. Holiday House, 1964. Caldecott Honor Book.

A repetitive story about impossible things that happen followed by the statement, "rain makes applesauce," used repeatedly. Illustrations depict that rain does make apples grow for applesauce.

Raindrops. Provide water, colored chalk, and freezer or finger paint paper (paper with a slick finish). Sprinkle water over paper or hold paper in rain for a few seconds. Draw with different colors of chalk all through the "raindrops." Allow to dry. Spray with nonaerosol hair spray as a fixative. (I,SG)

Additional rain titles:

Kalan, Robert. *Rain.* Illustrated by Donald Crews. Greenwillow, 1978.

Spier, Peter. *Peter Spier's Rain.* Doubleday, 1982.

Tresselt, Alvin. *Raindrop Splash.* Illustrated by Leonard Weisgard. Lothrop, Lee and Shepard, 1946. Caldecott Honor Book.

Apple printing. Have available apples, tempera paint, and newsprint. Cut apple in half lengthwise. Also, cut one crosswise if desired. Brush tempera on apple then print on paper. Variation: Use apple stencils to do apple stenciling designs on placemats, potholders, or other items. For stenciling on materials use acrylic or stenciling paint. (I,SG)

Additional apple titles:

Aliki. *The Story of Johnny Appleseed.* Prentice-Hall, 1963.

Barrett, Judith. *An Apple a Day.* Illustrated by Tim Lewis. Atheneum, 1973.

Hogrogian, Nonny. *Apples.* Macmillan, 1972.

Orbach, Ruth. *Apple Pigs.* Collins Publishers, 1977.

Programming notes: In the fall as part of the "signs of fall" unit, develop a theme around apples. In addition to ideas suggested above, provide some of the following activities:

- Use cooking experiences: applesauce, apple pie, candied apples, or apple salad. Or have an apple for snack.

- Visit an apple orchard to pick apples, or buy apples at an open air market.

- Have an apple bobbing contest. See who can get an apple with his teeth as they are floated in tub or pan of water.

Sendak, Maurice. **Where the Wild Things Are.** Harper & Row, 1963. Caldecott Medal Award.

A story of Max and his dreams when he was sent to bed without supper. Max encounters friendly monsters and an exciting adventure.

Masks. Provide grocery bags, crayons or felt tipped markers, and yarn. Using grocery bags, make masks to slip over head. Use your imagination. Make the wildest thing possible. Use crayons, magic markers, yarn, or a combination of materials. Cut out eyes so the "monster" can see with his mask on. (SG)

Masks. Have available pizza or cake rounds, tagboard, crayons, markers, yarn, and 12-inch rulers for each child. Use cardboard, pizza or cake rounds 12 to 14 inches in diameter as a base. To make the mask the size of the round, draw around the round on a piece of tagboard. On the tagboard have child draw the scariest monster possible. Add ears and yarn for the hair, if desired. Cut out the tagboard monster and glue on to the round. Use the ruler as a handle to hold the mask in front of face. Tape the ruler securely to the back of the round. Be sure to position the ruler so that the mask will be in the correct position when held up. Half of the ruler should extend beyond the mask to serve as a handle or holder. Note: Purchase inexpensive rulers or secure free advertising rulers. (SG,LG)

Hand puppet. Provide fabric crayons, newsprint, plain fabric (such as broadcloth), iron, needle, and thread. Use fabric crayons to draw monster on newsprint. Keep in mind the size appropriate for a hand puppet. With hot iron, transfer the drawing to fabric as directed on the fabric crayon instructions. Make the back of the puppet by cutting a second thickness of material as the monster transfer is cut out. Be sure to leave a half-inch allowance around the edge of the monster. Turn the puppet wrong side out. Stitch around the edges leaving the bottom open. Clip and turn. Note: Fabric with polyester content makes a better transfer. Stitch puppets on sewing machine to make them more sturdy. (SG)

Monster pillow. Have available crayons, newsprint, plain fabric (such as broadcloth), iron, needles, thread, and fiber fill stuffing. Stuffed animals and pillows are very appealing to school-age children. Make pillows square, rectangular, or round or the shape of the monster. Determine the shape and size. Draw monster on the newsprint with fabric crayons. Place drawing on fabric in appropriate place. Transfer by pressing with hot iron as fabric crayon instructions suggest. Cut double thickness of fabric leaving about a half-inch for seam allowance. Turn wrong side out and stitch. Leave a small opening on one side to stuff with fiber fill. Clip and turn. Stuff with fiber fill to desired fullness. Close opening and slip stitch. Note: Fabric crayon transfers more vividly to fabrics with part polyester content. (SG)

34 / LET'S CREATE

Programming notes: Use the art ideas plus the creative dramatics, music, and cooking experiences suggested in this guide to extend children's experiences with *Where the Wild Things Are.* A single activity may be used for a short program or the completion of a number of activities may take several days. Also, acquaint children with Maurice Sendak and some of his other works. Children respond favorably to Sendak's work and find his life and interests in illustrating fairy and folk tales as a child most interesting.

Shaw, Charles. **It Looked Like Spilt Milk.** Harper & Row, 1947. Out of print.

White shapes on dark blue illustrate this story. Shapes look like spilt milk and other things but they all turn out to be clouds in the sky. Illustrations are torn paper shapes.

Straw painting. Use diluted white tempera paint, drinking straws and dark colored construction paper. Place a small drop of white tempera on paper. Hold straw over paint and blow air through the straw. The air will spread the paint in a variety of directions. Decide what the shape looks like. Have children name their pictures. Repeat process as many times as desired. (I,SG,LG)

Blot painting. Provide dark blue construction paper and white tempera paint. Fold blue paper in half. Open paper and drop several small blobs of paint near the center of the paper. Close and rub. Open and decide what the picture looks like. Have children label their picture by saying, "It looks like ...." (SG,LG)

Torn paper collage. Use white paper for tearing and dark construction paper for background. Tear white paper in desired shapes. Children enjoy tearing planned shapes or tearing freely and then naming their creation. Glue torn pictures to dark background. Decide what the picture looks like and label it. (SG,LG)

"It Looks Like ..." book. Combine several pictures from one child or pictures from several children in a book. Secure spine with staples or punch two holes in the side and tie together with yarn. Leave the book wordless or write the name of the picture on the page. Share the book with the group. (I,SG)

"It Looks Like ..." bulletin board. Display pictures made by any of the techniques suggested above for a classroom or library bulletin board. Include the caption "It Looks Like ..." Label each picture with the appropriate identification supplied by the artist. (SG,LG)

Additional cloud titles:

De Paola, Tomie. *The Cloud Book.* Holiday House, 1975.

Spier, Peter. *Dreams.* Doubleday, 1986.

Programming notes: Experiences with this title might also include study and observation of clouds.

Spier, Peter. **Noah's Ark.** Doubleday, 1977. Caldecott Medal Award.

Humorous account of the story of Noah's Ark. Delightfully detailed illustrations. One finds new things and new humor each time he or she looks at the illustrations of this book.

Noah's Ark. Provide tagboard, shoe box, construction paper, empty thread spools, and markers or paints. Encourage children to look at the illustrations of the Ark by Spier in order to glean ideas for constructing their model of the Ark. Use part or all of the shoe box as a base on which to glue the sides of the Ark. Using tagboard, make animals to go in the Ark. Be sure to make two of each. To help animals stand, glue them to the side of an empty thread spool or use a tagboard loop made by stapling a small strip of tagboard together to form a loop. The size of the loop needed will depend upon the size of the animal. Note: School-age children love to construct and make three-dimensional things. This activity could take several days. It can involve as many children as might be interested. (I,SG)

Animal masks. Use paper plates, crayons, paints or magic markers, construction paper, glue and other things like yarn. Cut place for eyes. Decorate plate to look like animals on the

Ark. Tie on with yarn or use elastic stapled to each side to hold masks on. Be sure to make two of each. (I,SG)

Spier, Peter. **Oh, Were They Ever Happy!** Doubleday, 1978.

Mother and father leave for the day and the children paint the house with all the colors they could find in the garage. Oh, what a mess but oh, what fun. Beautiful watercolor illustrations.

Color mix. Provide a sponge, medicine droppers, several colors of diluted tempera, and heavy white paper. With sponge, wet the entire surface of the paper. Use medicine droppers to drop several colors on wet paper. Watch colors spread. Some will run together to make new colors. (I,SG)

Watercolor painting. Use commercial watercolors. Paint on white paper. Allow colors to run together. Give children time to experiment with watercolors and to be creative. Share techniques for painting with watercolors. For example, to prevent colors from running together one must dry before another one is applied. (I,SG)

Spier, Peter. **Star-Spangled Banner.** Doubleday, 1973.

The words to the song are illustrated. The illustrations are packed with action and accurate details from history.

Make a flag. Display an American flag. Provide red, white, and blue tempera paint and large pieces of newsprint. Have children paint an American flag. (I,SG)

Make a flag. Provide red, white, and blue construction paper and gum backed stars. Use a large piece of white paper for the background. Glue on the blue background for the stars. Add the stars and the red stripes. Be sure the correct number of stars and stripes are used.

Steig, William. **Sylvester and the Magic Pebble.** Simon and Schuster, 1969. Caldecott Medal Award.

A magic pebble causes Sylvester, a pebble collecting donkey, to turn into a rock. As a rock he experiences the changing seasons. The seasons are beautifully illustrated. The story has a happy ending when the magic pebble is placed on the rock and Sylvester wishes to become himself again.

Spring, fall, summer, or winter scenes. Use white construction paper or other available art paper and tempera paint. Apply paint with one of the following: cotton swabs, small sponges clipped to clothespins, small paint brushes, or "dobbers" made by attaching a cotton ball in a square of material to the end of a pencil with a rubber band. Using appropriate colors, have children paint a scene for each season or have them select the season they wish to illustrate. Note: For spring, add white to regular colors to create pastels. (I,SG)

Collage. Supply construction paper (including brown), assorted colors of tissue paper, and pencils with erasers. Make a picture of trees in the fall, summer, or spring. Make a tree trunk from construction paper. Use tissue paper for leaves: yellow, red, orange for fall; green, white, pink for spring. Put dots of glue on the paper where you wish for the leaves and/or blossoms to be. Twist small 1-by-1-inch pieces of tissue paper on the eraser end of a pencil. Release the twisted tissue paper in a dot of glue. Continue until complete. (I,SG)

Stone critters. Use the same ideas as suggested for stone critters in this chapter for a follow-up activity for Marcia Brown's *Stone Soup.*

Programming notes: School-age children enjoy collections. Try some of the following activities to develop a theme on rocks:

- Invite someone to share their rock or precious stone collection.

- Find out about rocks and precious stones unique to your given area.

- Go on a walk to collect stones. Try to find a brook or stream to find smooth rocks for stone critters.

- Use games that require the use of stones such as hopscotch.

36 / LET'S CREATE

Tresselt, Alvin. **Hide and Seek Fog.** Illustrated by Roger A. Duvoisin. Lothrop, Lee and Shepard, 1965.

Depicts a foggy day at the seashore. The children responded more positively to the fog than their parents when it stayed for three days in a little village on Cape Cod where they were vacationing. The hazy, gray illustrations convey the mystery of a foggy day.

Foggy scene. Have available a variety of colors of construction paper including some gray and black and waxed paper. Paste paper cut outs onto a gray background. Glue a layer of waxed paper over the scene. Frame by cutting a frame from the same size construction paper as the background piece. Measure 1 inch from the edge on all sides, mark, and cut out.[5] (I,SG)

Tresselt, Alvin. **Johnny Maple-Leaf.** Illustrated by Roger A. Duvoisin. Lothrop, Lee and Shepard, 1948.

Johnny Maple-Leaf is followed through the seasons. An excellent story to help children understand what happens to leaves during the changing seasons from spring to winter.

Leaf melt. Have available waxed paper, crayon shavings, newspaper, construction paper, and iron. Go on a walk to collect leaves. Place several leaves on a piece of waxed paper. Sprinkle crayon shavings over leaves. Cover with another piece of waxed paper. Place between several thicknesses of newspaper. Press with hot iron. Frame with a 1-inch construction paper frame. Note: Use old wax crayons for shaving. Shave crayons with the open edge of scissors or use a plastic vegetable grater. (I,SG)

Leaf mobile. Provide clear plastic adhesive and a coat hanger or dowel sticks of varying lengths. Collect a variety of leaves. Press some of the leaves collected over night in a catalog or under something heavy. Place leaves one at a time between clear plastic adhesive. Trim to within 1/8 inch of the leaf. Punch a hole in the top of each leaf. Hang from a coat hanger, stick, or other mobile type arrangement with different lengths of string. (I,SG)

Leaf rubbing. Have on hand newsprint, cardboard, rubber cement, and rubbing crayons. Go on a nature walk in the fall. Collect different sizes and shapes of leaves. Mount a few on a board, such as shirt board, with rubber cement. Be sure the vein side of the leaf is up. Place a piece of newsprint over the board and leaves. Rub with the flat side of a crayon. Identify the maple leaves. (I,SG)

Tresselt, Alvin. **A Thousand Lights and Fireflies.** Illustrated by John Moodie. Parent's Magazine Press, 1965.

Beautifully illustrated contrast of the country and city in illustrations of pastels.

Pastels or colored chalk. You will need pastels or colored chalk, drawing paper, and nonaerosol hair spray. Make your own chalk drawing. Spray with nonaerosol hair spray as a fixative. Note: For brighter colors, wet paper with sugar and water mixture. The mixture serves as a fixative. (I,SG)

Tresselt, Alvin. **White Snow, Bright Snow.** Illustrated by Roger A. Duvoisin. Lothrop, Lee and Shepard, 1947. Caldecott Medal Award.

Depicts the world waiting for the season's first snowfall. Bold black and white illustrations show the first snowflakes and the town after the first snowfall.

Snow scene. Provide white tempera, dark construction paper, and sharpened pencils with erasers. Dip a pencil point (for thin dots) or eraser (for thicker dots) into white tempera paint. Press down and pick up on dark paper to make snow scene. Note: Use cotton swabs as an alternate method of applying paint. (I,SG)

Udry, Janice May. **A Tree Is Nice.** Illustrated by Marc Simont. Harper & Row, 1956. Caldecott Medal Award.

Brilliant tempera illustrations of the changes of a tree and its surroundings through the seasons of the year. The book is tall and vertical in shape.

Torn paper collage. Use construction paper for this activity. Make a tree in the fall, spring, or summer. Use construction paper to draw and cut or tear a tree trunk. Mount the tree trunk on construction paper. Tear leaves from appropriate colors of construction paper for the chosen season. Glue torn paper leaves on the tree. (I,SG)

Sponge painting. Use manila drawing paper or construction paper, sponges clipped with clothespins, and tempera paint. Make a picture of trees in fall, spring, summer or winter. Use tempera paint with colors appropriate to the season to be illustrated. Apply paint with sponges, one sponge per color. Paint the tree trunk with brush-like strokes, the leaves with up and down stamping motion. (I,SG)

Programming notes: Use the ideas here and the ideas for Alvin Tresselt's *Johnny Maple-Leaf* for a seasonal theme like "signs of fall" or "trees in the fall." See Arbor Day celebration suggestions for additional extensions of titles about trees and leaves.

Williams, Vera B. **A Chair for My Mother.** Greenwillow, 1982. Caldecott Honor Book.

A little girl, her mother, and her grandmother save their money to buy a comfortable armchair for the mother, after all their furniture is burned in a fire. The colorful illustrations are done in watercolors. Each page is framed by a painted border. The title of the book appears in mosaic style.

Mosaic letters. Have available construction paper, pencils, scissors, and glue. Encourage children to practice making their names, mosaic style. Outline each name with block letters. Glue small pieces of paper to each letter, covering the whole letter. (I,SG)

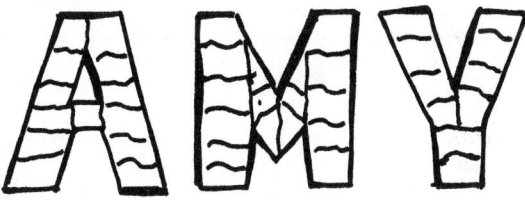

Picture frames or borders. Provide watercolors and white construction paper. After viewing this book, children may enjoy making borders for the pictures they draw or paint. (I,SG)

Yashima, Taro. **Crow Boy.** Viking, 1955. Caldecott Honor Book.

A shy Japanese mountain boy is a lonely outcast at school. An understanding teacher recognizes his potential and helps him gain self-confidence and respect. The illustrations become bolder as the boy gains confidence.

Japanese origami. Consult Japanese origami directions from books of crafts from other lands or have someone from Japan visit and demonstrate the fascinating technique. Choose things that the children could easily make using this paper folding technique. (I,SG,LG)

Additional titles from Japan:

Bang, Molly. *The Paper Crane.* Greenwillow, 1985.

Yashima, Taro. *Umbrella.* Viking, 1958.

Programming notes: Crow Boy can be used independently or in connection with the Japanese New Year celebration theme. School-age children like to find out about other lands. A travel unit with focus on individual country themes is very appropriate for school-age children. Some suggestions include the following:

- Consult *A to Zoo: Subject Access to Children's Picture Books* and other selections tools to find titles available on a given country.

- Present fictional as well as factual information on each country.
- Learn about the geography, customs, dress, food, and other things unique to the country.
- Play games children in the chosen country play.
- Invite appropriate resource persons to visit and take field trips.
- Spend several days on a theme.

Zion, Gene. **Really Spring.** Illustrated by Margaret B. Graham. Harper & Row, 1956.
    The children paint their own spring when they become tired of waiting for spring to come.
    Paint a springtime picture. Use small paint brushes or cotton swabs to paint a springtime picture. Mix white with bright colors to make pastels. Use pinks, yellows, and greens. (I,SG)

NOTES

[1] Jean Warren, *Crafts,* illustrated by Susan True (Palo Alto, Calif.: Monday Morning Books, 1983), 6.

[2] Michele Borba and Dan Ungaro, *Bookends* (Carthage, Ill.: Good Apple, 1982), 66.

[3] Charlotte Huck, *Children's Literature in the Elementary School* (New York: Holt, Rinehart and Winston, 1977), 643.

[4] Michele Borba and Dan Ungaro, *Bookends* (Carthage, Ill.: Good Apple, 1982), 117.

[5] Borba and Ungaro, *Bookends*, 88.

3
LET'S PRETEND
Children's Literature and Creative Dramatics

Acting out their concepts of the world around them, pretending and dramatizing, is second nature to most children. One of the most natural ways children respond to their literature is through creative dramatics. Children need opportunities to interpret their literature in ways that are familiar and real to them. As they act out their understanding of characters, plot, action, mood, and setting of the literature it becomes more real to them.

Not every school-age child will choose to participate in drama, but many will. Those who do not wish to be the actors may assist with props, scenery, or sound effects. With some thought and planning a part may be found for everyone who wishes to participate. With very little experience and minimal encouragement from teachers, given the opportunity children will initiate their own "plays." They will seek stories and verse to dramatize or make up their own.

VALUES OF USING LITERATURE BASED CREATIVE DRAMATIC ACTIVITIES

- To provide avenues for creative expression and individual interpretation.

- To develop listening and speaking skills.

- To develop ability to recall in an ordered sequence.

- To introduce new words into the spoken vocabulary.

- To contribute to the growth in the ability to empathize.

- To provide therapy for shy or troubled children by providing roles where they can become someone or something other than themselves.

- To be aware of and appreciate the magic and power of words.

- To develop a strong sense of story.

TECHNIQUES FOR CREATIVE DRAMATIC ACTIVITIES

- Select appropriate literature for young children.

- Present the literature in clear, vivid ways several times so the children can become familiar with the story, action, characters, feeling, and other elements unique to the chosen verse or prose.

- Discuss the story, characters, sequence of events, and props needed briefly before dramatization.

- Plan how dramatization will be carried out.

- Choose volunteers to act the parts. Other children can be the audience; they may provide words or sound effects or just enjoy the dramatization.

- Allow time for all the children who wish to have a turn to play a part.

- Select new actors by allowing the ones just finished, one at a time, to select someone from the audience to play their parts.

- Leave costumes and props at a minimum; most should be left to the viewers' imagination.

- Allow children to be spontaneous and to use language and body gestures comfortable to them.

- Encourage children to improvise but keep dialogue and actions true to the sense of the characters and theme.

- Encourage children to use expression.

- Do not overuse dramatization, causing the children to become tired of it.

- Dramatize a story when the children have reacted vividly and want the story to continue.

- Allow children to initiate and plan their own dramatizations.

KINDS OF LITERATURE FOR DRAMATIZATION

- Stories with a definite plot, characters, and action. Interesting characters, repetition, and easy sequence of events are important.

- Stories should be free of actual violence and ultimately have a safe, happy ending.

- Chapters or parts of a story instead of the complete story can be used.

- Situations within a story may be posed or acted out.

- Literature involving only characters and action, such as nursery rhymes and poetry.

- Stories with cumulative action.

METHODS OF EVALUATION

- Observe for an increased request and circulation of books, stories, and authors/illustrators used.

- Note children's interest, participation, and requests for repeated or similar activities.

- Present appropriate stories and poetry to children and let them plan and carry out dramatization on their own after experiencing teacher directed activities.

- Observe children initiating their own creative dramatics, plays, puppet shows, and the like.

CHILDREN'S LITERATURE AND CREATIVE DRAMATICS

Bible Stories

Many Bible stories lend themselves to creative dramatics. Simple costumes of the time may be used, or children may wish to make puppets to represent the characters in the story. Children also like to pose a scene or several scenes of a story.

More and more Bible stories are being published in single picture book form. An excellent selection tool for identifying Bible story titles is Patricia Pearl's *Religious Books for Children*. One of the best ways to present a Bible story is to read the story from the Bible in a modern day version like the *Good News Bible, the Bible in Today's English Version*. After the story is read, have the children identify the characters and tell the story in their own words.

Some of many Bible stories that lend themselves to acting out include:

The Christmas Story	The Story of Ruth
The Good Neighbor (Good Samaritan)	The Helpful Friends
The Loving Father (Prodigal Son)	The Blind Man
The Boy Who Shared His Lunch	The Thankful Leper
Joseph and His Coat of Many Colors	David and Jonathan
The Lost Coin	The Lost Sheep

De Paola, Tomie. **The Christmas Pageant.** Winston, 1981.
   The Christmas story with cut out puppets to color and assemble for a Christmas Pageant. The story includes the preparation of Joseph and Mary for Jesus' birth, his birth in Bethlehem, and the visit of the shepherds and wise men.
   Puppet Show. Color and cut out the puppets provided in the book. Mount on popsicle sticks with tape or glue. Prepare a puppet stage; ideas are given in the book. Select puppeteers and a reader. As the story is read, puppets appear. (I,SG)
   Flannel board story. The same cutouts can be backed with felt or flocked wallpaper. Glue a small strip of either on the back of the cutout. This will allow the characters to adhere to a flannel board. As the story is read or told, children may place the characters on the board. (I,SG)

De Paola, Tomie. **The Story of the Three Wise Kings.** Putnam's Sons, 1983.
   The story of the wise men who went to Bethlehem to see Jesus is retold. Their names, Melchoir, Gaspar, and Balthazar, are given. Simply told, beautifully illustrated, and easily dramatized.
   Dramatize the story. Select children to be the wise men, Joseph, and Mary. Use a doll for baby Jesus. Prepare gifts. Pantomime the story as it is read or told by a narrator. (SG)

Lindvall, Ella K. Joseph and His Brothers. Illustrated by Chris Molan. Moody, 1982.

Beautifully illustrated version of Joseph's boyhood story. Joseph was favored by his father but sold into slavery by his brothers.

Dramatize the story. Use a brightly colored coat for Joseph. No other props needed. Characters may speak or act out the story as a narrator tells or reads it. (SG)

Fables

Fables are fun to act out because of the brief story, few characters (usually animals), and cumulative events. Fables usually have a message or moral to the story. The story rather than the moral is more important to school-age children.

Brown, Marcia. Once a Mouse. Scribner, 1961. Caldecott Medal Award.

A delightful fable from India retells what happens when a hermit turns a frightened mouse first into a cat, then a dog, and finally a tiger. Illustrations are done with woodcuts.

Act out the story. Choose players for the different characters and act out the story. No props are needed. (SG)

Additional fables:

Aesop. *Aesop's Fables.* Illustrated by Heidi Holder. Viking, 1981.

Caldecott, Randolph. *The Caldecott Aesop, a Facsimile of the 1883 Edition.* Doubleday, 1978.

Galdone, Paul. *The Monkey and the Crocodile.* Seabury Press, 1969.

_____ . *The Town Mouse and the Country Mouse.* McGraw-Hill, 1971.

LaFontaine, Jean de. *The Hare and the Tortoise.* Illustrated by Brian Wildsmith. Watts, 1966.

_____ . *The Lion and the Rat.* Illustrated by Brian Wildsmith. Watts, 1963.

_____ . *The North Wind and the Sun.* Illustrated by Brian Wildsmith. Watts, 1964.

Folk Tales and Fairy Tales

Folk tales and fairy tales work well for creative dramatics because they are familiar stories and have the repetition and cumulative qualities that make them easy to remember and dramatize.

Little Red Riding Hood. Illustrated by Paul Galdone. McGraw-Hill, 1974.

A traditional presentation of the story of the little girl who encountered a wolf on her way to grandmother's house. Little Red Riding Hood and grandmother escape from the wolf. The ending is happy and the illustrations are very appealing.

Act out the story. Have the children take turns portraying the characters in the story. The characters include the grandmother, Little Red Riding Hood, the wolf, and the woodcutters. (SG,LG)

Tape the story. Have the children tape their telling of the story. Play the stories back for some unique listening experiences. (I,SG)

Make puppets. Use paper bags, finger or sock puppets to act out each character of the story. If commercial puppets are not available, children can make their own. Directions for making puppets can be found in the "Let's Create" chapter. (SG)

Perrault, Charles. **Cinderella.** Illustrated by Marcia Brown. Scribner, 1954. Caldecott Medal Award.
The traditional story illustrated in very flowing, fairylike fashion. Cinderella is turned from a poor maiden to a beautiful Princess by her Fairy Godmother. She goes to the ball and is chosen to dance with the Prince. At the stroke of twelve, she runs from the palace losing her glass slipper before she turns back into the poor maiden. When the Prince finds her, the slipper is a perfect fit.

Act out the story. Choose players, props, and review the story. Select and act out the most important scenes. (SG)

Tape record feelings. Have children pretend to be the prince, Cinderella, and other characters. Tape some of their feelings before and after the ball. (I,SG)

The Three Billy Goats Gruff. Illustrated by Paul Galdone. Seabury Press, 1973.

The Three Billy Goats Gruff. Illustrated by Susan Blair. Holt, Rinehart and Winston, 1963.
Traditional version of the story of the three billy goats and the old troll. The billy goats must travel over the bridge where the mean old troll lives in order to find a hillside with green grass.

Act out the story. Use a table for the bridge for the troll to hide under and the goats to cross over. Children not playing the characters may add appropriate sound effects. Designate an area for the hill with green grass. Only four characters are needed. (SG)

Add masks. Make large cardboard flats for the three goats and the troll. Cut out the face and a place for the hands. Each character will use his flat as he appears in the play. (SG)

Additional folk tales:

CHICKEN LITTLE

Chicken Licken. Retold by Kenneth McLeish. Illustrated by Jutta Ash. Bradbury, 1972.

Henny Penny. Illustrated by Paul Galdone. Seabury Press, 1968.

THE GINGERBREAD MAN

The Gingerbread Boy. Illustrated by Paul Galdone. Seabury Press, 1975.

Johnny-Cake. Illustrated by William Stobbs. Viking, 1973.

Johnney Cake, Ho! Retold by Ruth Sawyer. Illustrated by Robert McCloskey. Viking, 1953.

GOLDILOCKS AND THE THREE BEARS

The Three Bears. Illustrated by Paul Galdone. Seabury Press, 1972.

The Three Bears. Illustrated by Feodor S. Rojankovsky. Western Publishing Co., 1967.

LITTLE RED RIDING HOOD

Little Red Riding Hood. Illustrated by Bernadette Watts. Collins, 1969.

Red Riding Hood. Retold by Beatrice Schenk De Regniers. Illustrated by Edward Gorey. Atheneum, 1972.

THE MAGIC PORRIDGE POT

The Magic Porridge Pot. Illustrated by Paul Galdone. Seabury Press, 1976.

Strega Nona. Retold and illustrated by Tomie De Paola. Prentice-Hall, 1975.

THE THREE LITTLE PIGS

The Three Little Pigs. Illustrated by Paul Galdone. Seabury Press, 1970.

The Three Little Pigs. Illustrated by William Pene du Bois. Viking, 1962.

Nursery Rhymes

Any nursery rhyme that is narrative in nature can be acted out. Children may dress in character, make and/or collect props to use, or without costumes or props, act out rhymes in charade fashion. Nursery rhymes fun to act out include:

Little Miss Muffet	Cat and the Fiddle
Jack and Jill	Three Little Kittens
Old King Cole	Little Bo Peep
Sing a Song of Sixpence	Mary Had a Little Lamb
Jack Be Nimble	Baa, Baa Black Sheep
Little Jack Horner	Hickory Dickory Dock
Little Boy Blue	Jack Sprat

Jack Be Nimble. Use a short unlighted candle in a nonbreakable candle holder or use a candle made from construction paper.

Little Miss Muffet. Have a small foot stool for the tuffet. Other props may include an oversized bowl and spoon and a construction paper black spider suspended with a rubber band.

Three Little Kittens. Use actual mittens as props, choose three kittens and mother cat. Have a narrator read or say the rhyme as the characters act it out.

Titles of nursery rhyme collections:

De Angeli, Marguerite. *Marguerite De Angeli's Book of Nursery and Mother Goose Rhymes.* Doubleday, 1954.

De Paola, Tomie. *Mother Goose.* Putnam's Sons, 1985.

Fujikawa, Gyo. *Mother Goose.* Grosset and Dunlap, 1981.

The Random House Book of Mother Goose. Selected and illustrated by Arnold Lobel. Random House, 1986.

Rojankovsky, Feodor. *Tall Book of Mother Goose.* Harper & Row, 1942.

Wildsmith, Brian. *Brian Wildsmith's Mother Goose.* Watts, 1965.

Wright, Blanche. *The Real Mother Goose.* Rand McNally, 1978.

Children's Picture Book Stories

Aardema, Verna. **Why Mosquitoes Buzz in People's Ears.** Illustrated by Leo Dillon and Diane Dillon. Dial, 1975. Caldecott Medal Award.
  Mosquito tells Iguana a foolish story. Iguana puts sticks in his ears to keep from hearing. Not hearing causes a series of mishaps. The unique illustrations depict the cumulative story with movement and humor.

Gossip. Play a gossip game. Whisper a message or phrase in one child's ear and have that child pass it on to the next child by whispering it in his or her ear. Repeat around the circle. Have the last child repeat the message or phrase. Compare it with the original message. (LG)

Brown, Margaret Wise. **The Runaway Bunny.** Illustrated by Clement Hurd. Harper & Row, 1942.

A tender story of a mother's love for her child. No matter what Little Bunny wants to become, his mother will follow him to protect and love him.

Creative dramatics activity. Select someone to play Mother Bunny. Different children can pretend to be Little Bunny when he becomes different things. Make name cards for Mother Bunny and the Little Bunnies. (SG)

De Regniers, Beatrice Schenk. **May I Bring a Friend?** Illustrated by Beni Montresor. Atheneum, 1964.

The king invites a boy to visit him. Each day the boy brings a different friend from the zoo. When the queen asks the king if the boy can bring a friend the king responds by saying "My dear, my dear, any friend of our friend I welcome here."

May I bring a friend? game. Use words from the story for a game. When a child's name is mentioned, he or she supplies the name of the friend he or she plans to bring. Children may chant:

The King and Queen invited <u>child's name</u>
To come to their house on <u>day</u> for <u>event</u> .
I told the Queen and the Queen told the King
<u>child's name</u> had a friend he/she wanted to bring.
The King told the Queen,
"My dear, my dear, any friend of our friend,
I welcome here."
So <u>child's name</u> brought his/her friend, <u>name</u> .

Note: Make the chant difficult by requiring the child chosen to name only animals of a certain category, birds, or names that begin with a certain letter. For example, name only friends that begin with "A" (Amy, Albert, Alice, etc.). (SG,LG)

Duvoisin, Roger. **Donkey-Donkey.** Parent's Magazine Press, 1968.

Donkey-Donkey was not happy with the way he looked. He did not like his ears. After he tried ears like some of his animal friends, he decided he wasn't so bad after all.

Variation of creative dramatics. Choose children to be the various characters of the story. Head bands with different types of ears that Donkey-Donkey wanted can be used as props. (SG,LG)

Eastman, P. D. **Are You My Mother?** Random House, 1960.

A story about a bird who hatches while his mother is out finding food. The baby bird falls out of the nest and goes in search of his mother. He encounters several animals and other things that turn out not to be his mother. He is returned to his nest just in time to see his mother when she returns with his food. A very popular beginning reading book.

Character charades. Choose one child to be the baby bird and others to be the other characters. The baby bird will be "it." Secretly give the other children the name of a character. Have each child act out the character assigned to him or her in charade fashion. Have the child give one hint at a time when the baby bird asks "Are you my mother?" The baby bird should try to guess each character as well as his or her mother. When characters are guessed correctly they are eliminated. When baby bird finds his or her mother, that person becomes "it." Assign characters and play the game again. (SG)

46 / LET'S PRETEND

Flack, Marjorie. **Ask Mr. Bear.** Macmillan, 1932.
    A little boy asks lots of animals for suggestions for his mother's birthday. His mother had eggs, a pillow, cheese, a blanket, and milk and cream. The best suggestion of all came from Mr. Bear. He suggested a great big bear hug.
    Act out the story. Select children to be the various characters. Use pictures or the real item that each character suggests as a reminder of what each would contribute. This story is more appealing to the kindergarten and first grade than older children. (SG)

Guilfoile, Elizabeth. **Nobody Listens to Andrew.** Illustrated by Mary Stevens. Follet, 1957.
    Everyone was too busy to listen to Andrew when he tried to tell them that a bear was in his room. Family members and community helpers respond negatively to Andrew when he tells them about the bear for they do not have time. When they see, a big commotion results.
    Act out the story. Have volunteers be the characters of the story. This story calls for a lot of excitement and expression—real acting. (SG)

Holarbird, Katharine. **Angelina on Stage.** Illustrated by Helen Craig. Potter Publishers, 1986.
    Angelina and her cousin, Henry, are chosen to be in an adult musical. She is a fairy and he is an elf. Angelina is jealous of Henry because everyone thinks he is so cute, but she becomes concerned for him when she realizes how nervous he is. The characters are mice. The text and illustrations are a vivid recreation of the theater world. Theater vocabulary is included in the text.
    Play productions. Encourage children to present their own plays. Nursery rhymes and nursery tales are good, familiar texts for beginners. For example, use Tomie De Paola's *Favorite Nursery Tales* (Putnam's Sons, 1986). Familiar stories are included in this collection and the illustrations are simple. Children can easily use the illustrations for ideas for stick or paper bag puppets. (SG)

Keats, Ezra Jack. **Louie.** Greenwillow, 1975.
    The children put on a puppet show. They give Louie the puppet he responded to.
    Puppet show. Make your own puppets from paper bags, paper plates, paper maché, or other materials of your choice. Have a puppet show. (SG)

    Programming notes: If children cannot come up with a script of their own for the puppet show, suggest that they use a familiar fairy or folk tale. Fairy and folk tales are good to use because of their cumulative qualities and familiar story line.

Mayer, Mercer. **You're the Scaredy Cat.** Parent's Magazine Press, 1974.
    Two young brothers camp out in the backyard. Older brother tries to scare younger brother with a monster story.
    Scary story. Make up the scariest story possible to share with classmates. Use imagination and sense of adventure. Tape some of the stories. (I,SG)

    Additional title:

Mayer, Mercer. *There's A Nightmare in My Closet.* Dial, 1968.

Schwartz, Alvin. **In a Dark, Dark Room and Other Scary Stories.** Illustrated by Dirk Zimmer. Harper & Row, 1984.
    A collection of short stories for the young reader. Stories include "The Teeth," "In the Graveyard," "The Green Ribbon," "In a Dark, Dark Room," and "The Ghost of John" plus many more. A good book for beginning readers. The foreword provides pointers for telling or reading scary stories, and notes on the origin of the stories are included.
    Read the stories. Darken the room and have children read or tell the stories. Remember to set the mood and present the stories slowly and quietly. (SG,LG)

Share original stories. Encourage children to create their own stories. Have them write them down. They may choose to illustrate their stories. Note: Kindergarten and first grade children have vivid imaginations but will need help to write down their stories. They may wish to record their story on a tape rather than write it down. (SG)

Sendak, Maurice. **Where the Wild Things Are.** Harper & Row, 1963. Caldecott Medal Award.

A story of Max and his dreams when he was sent to his room without supper. In his dreams, Max encounters wild but friendly monsters.

Creative activity. Several days can be spent on this story. Include art and music activities. (SG,LG)

Masks. Make masks for the monsters and Max. Using grocery bags, make masks to slip over characters' heads. Use your imagination. Use an unlimited number of monsters, the wildest possible. Use crayons, magic markers, yarn, or a combination of materials (SG,LG). Additional ideas are found in the "Let's Create" chapter.

Music. Listen to available music. Select the wildest, loudest music possible for the wild rumpus. Choose someone to read or tell the story. Let the play begin! (I,SG,LG)

Programming notes: See suggestions in the other activity chapters in this guide to help develop a theme on monsters or works of Maurice Sendak.

Slobodkina, Esphyr. **Caps for Sale.** Addison-Wesley, 1940.

A story of a peddler, some monkeys, and their monkey business. After a nap under a tree, the peddler awakes to find that his caps are gone. He looks up into the tree to find chattering monkeys, and on each monkey's head a cap.

Act out the story. Select a narrator, peddler, and monkeys. Props can be imaginary or real caps for the peddler. Use as many monkeys as there are children who wish to participate. This story works best for younger children. The story calls for the portrayal of a variety of emotions. (SG,LG)

4
LET'S MAKE MUSIC
Children's Literature and Creative Music Activities

Children readily respond to music of all kinds. They love to sing, play instruments, listen to music, and respond in creative ways such as dance and movement. School-age children enjoy nonsense songs and chants. A unique genre of children's literature includes single song picture books. Other titles and verses elicit musical accompaniment, sound effects, or movement interpretation.

Creative music activities extend children's experiences with their literature, help children become more aware and familiar with picture book versions of single songs, and give them another avenue for creative interpretations, expression, and individual response to their literature. Children nor teachers need to be musical to respond musically to children's literature. Given the opportunity, children will respond by singing or in some other way using music. Such response may spark an interest in a given type or mode of musical expression that may last a lifetime.

VALUES OF USING LITERATURE BASED CREATIVE MUSIC ACTIVITIES

- To develop listening skills.

- To develop ability to recall in an ordered sequence by singing songs.

- To introduce new vocabulary and new concepts through songs, use of musical instruments, and recorded music.

- To help children become sensitive to the beauty of music.

- To provide opportunities for relaxation and rhythmic responses.

- To provide a medium through which children find outlets for emotions.

- To provide opportunities for creativity as children are encouraged to make their own tunes, words, and/or rhythms.

TECHNIQUES FOR CREATIVE MUSIC ACTIVITIES

- Select literature that lends itself to musical response.

- Select single song picture books that have words and illustrations placed appropriately for easy singing and response.

- Select single song picture books that have the music printed at the end of the book for easy reference.

- Present the literature in an appropriate way (read aloud, storytelling, filmstrip, movie, recording).

- Identify possible ways to use music with the chosen literature.

- Allow child to hear the song of a single song picture book before expecting him to actively participate.

- Identify mood, rhythm, and other elements of the literature appropriate for musical response.

- Introduce instruments and appropriate techniques for their use to the children.

- Allow children to be creative and experiment with the music and musical instruments.

- Accept each child's individual response to music.

KINDS OF LITERATURE TO USE WITH MUSIC

- Picture books of single songs that call for singing along as the pictures are shown, or call for accompanying text with musical instruments.

- Literature such as poetry, wordless books, and stories for dramatization that lends itself to a choice of background music.

- Poetry and other literature that might be interpreted by dance and movement.

METHODS OF EVALUATION

- Observe for an increased interest and request for song books and other music related literature.

- Observe for spontaneous singing and setting words to music.

- Present appropriate stories and poems and allow the children to select the music or instruments to use with the literature.

- Ask such questions as: Do the children seem to enjoy the activity? Do they want to do more? Do they ask for more? Have these experiences sparked interest in musical instruments or other music related information?

CHILDREN'S LITERATURE AND CREATIVE MUSIC ACTIVITIES

Picture Books of Single Songs

Listed below are some ideas to use with selected single song picture books. One activity that can be used with almost all of the titles is to sing the song to accompany the illustrations. Only different or

50 / LET'S MAKE MUSIC

additional ideas will be suggested here. An additional list of single songs in picture books will be listed at the end of this section.

Adams, Adrienne. **I Know an Old Lady Who Swallowed a Fly.** Grosset and Dunlap, 1973.
Delightful folk song illustrated very appropriately. A cumulative song that can easily be remembered and sung.
Music activity. Make flannel board illustrations. Use flannel, dressmaker's pellon, or paper figures backed with flannel for flannel board characters. Sing the song as appropriate character is placed on the flannel board. Children may continue activity independently.
Teacher assistance is needed to make flannel or pellon illustrations. The pellon material works very well for flannel board characters; features may be drawn on this material with thin felt tipped watercolor pens. Children more easily make their own characters by drawing them on drawing paper then cutting the characters out and backing them with a strip of felt to help adhere to the flannel board. Tagboard or poster board is the best weight paper for characters. Use only a small amount of glue to mount flannel strips to the back of the characters. (SG,LG)

Adams, Adrienne. **This Old Man.** Grosset and Dunlap, 1975.
Counting rhyme set to music. The very familiar children's counting song. Each verse adds a number and corresponding number of items.
Music activity. Sing along as the illustrations are shown. Have children make posters or cards to illustrate each thing the old man caught. Use crayons, magic markers, or tempera paint to make the illustrations. Have children stand in front of the group as his number is sung. After singing the song, have the children stand in numerical order and sing the song again. Use the wave effect of showing the illustrations quickly as each item is repeated. Such as, "This old man, he caught one ... , two ... , three ... ," to the end. Repeat as many times as the children wish. (SG,LG)

Bangs, Edward. **Steven Kellogg's Yankee Doodle.** Illustrated by Steven Kellogg. Parent's Magazine Press, 1976.
Traditional patriotic song. Each line of the song is illustrated with full-page paintings filled with activity.
Parade. Make paper Yankee Doodle hats. For directions consult the "Let's Create" chapter. Have each child select a rhythm instrument. Form a parade line and have a parade. Wear hats and march to the music, playing the instruments and singing "Yankee Doodle." (LG)

Additional parade title:

Crews, Donald. *Parade.* Greenwillow, 1983.

Programming notes: Use this title and activities as part of the Independence Day celebration. For parade ideas, see Donald Crews's *Parade.* Younger children, kindergarten and first grade, will find this activity most appealing.

Child, Lydia Maria. **Over the River and Through the Wood.** Illustrated by Brinton Turkle. Coward, McCann, and Geoghegan, 1974.
Thanksgiving song with illustrations from the horse and sleigh period. Pictures and lines of the song correspond.
Jingle bells. Use jingle bells or sleigh bells to accompany the singing of "Over the River and Through the Wood." (LG)
Note: Jingle bells are small, round metal bells found in craft shops or included with rhythm band instruments. If secured from a craft shop, sew two or three on a band of elastic for wrist bells or to a long strip of fabric. When shaken, the bells will jingle, sounding like sleigh bells.

Programming notes: A perfect title to use at Thanksgiving.

Emberley, Barbara. **One Wide River to Cross.** Illustrated by Ed Emberley. Prentice-Hall, 1966. Caldecott Honor Book.

A picture book interpretation of an old folk song. Music is included in the book. A humorous adaptation of the Bible story, Noah's Ark. The song contains new words for each line of the verse plus "one wide river to cross" is repeated after each new line. Illustrated with black woodcuts against bright colors.

Responsive singing. Learn the song, "One Wide River to Cross." Sing the song instead of reading the words to the story. Have one child or the teacher sing the verse and the rest of the group chant the line "one wide river to cross" after each new line in the verse. Because of the "silly" verse, children will respond to this song. (SG,LG)

Programming notes: Use this title just for fun. The illustration technique is also an excellent example of the woodcut technique. Be sure to use it as an example when studying this technique.

Keats, Ezra Jack. **The Little Drummer Boy.** Macmillan, 1968.

Beautifully illustrated version of the song about a poor boy who gave his gift, music on his drum, to baby Jesus.

Drum. Use a drum to accompany this song at appropriate places. Children will become more familiar with the song as they decide when to use the drum sounds. (SG,LG)

Programming notes: Use this title as part of the Christmas celebration theme.

Peek, Merle. **Roll Over! A Counting Song.** Houghton-Mifflin, 1981.

The traditional fun song beginning with ten characters and ending with one in the bed, "At Last!" Words and illustrations compatible.

Sing along. Sing the song as the pages are turned. Children like to experiment with the song, singing the song more rapidly. Try singing the song in rounds by dividing the group first in half, one group beginning and the second group beginning after the first "roll over, roll over" line. The first group will drop out when they finish the song with the second group finishing the last line by themselves.

Singing in rounds is fun but requires more concentration. When the group perfects singing in two groups, try singing the song in rounds by dividing the group into three small groups. Again, because of the repetitiveness and nonsense children will enjoy singing this song. (LG)

Zemach, Margot. **Hush, Little Baby.** Dutton, 1976.

A lullaby with one verse building on another. Words and illustrations cover a two page spread for each line. Illustrations are pictures painted including some humor in each. Music to the song is included in the back of the book.

Melody bells. Write out the notes to the song on music lines. Color code the notes with corresponding notes on the melody bells, slip bells, or xylophone. Practice playing the melody to accompany the singing of the song. With a little practice children are able to play and sing the song or accompany the group singing of the song. Note: Use colored tape or small pieces of colored paper taped on for coding. (I,SG)

Zuromskis, Diane. **The Farmer in the Dell.** Little, Brown, & Co., 1978.

The familiar song from everyone's childhood. The song can be just sung or sung and played out.

Flannel board characters. Make flannel board characters to illustrate the song as children sing it. Consult Adrienne Adams's *I Know an Old Lady Who Swallowed a Fly* for ideas for making flannel board characters. (SG,LG)

Additional picture books of single songs (a selected list):

ANIMAL SONGS

Conover, Chris. **Six Little Ducks.** Crowell, 1976.

De Regniers, Beatrice Schenk. **Catch a Little Fox.** Illustrated by Brinton Turkle. Seabury Press, 1970.

Keats, Ezra Jack. **Over in the Meadow.** Words by O. A. Wadsworth. Scholastic Books, 1972.

Langstaff, John. **Over in the Meadow.** Illustrated by Feodor Rojankovsky. Harcourt, Brace, Jovanovich, 1973.

Quackenbush, Robert. **Pop Goes the Weasel and Yankee Doodle.** Lippincott, 1976.

Spier, Peter. **The Fox Went Out on a Chilly Night.** Music by Burl Ives. Doubleday, 1961.

CHRISTMAS SONGS

Broomfield, Robert. **The Twelve Days of Christmas.** McGraw-Hill, 1965.

De Paola, Tomie. **The Friendly Beasts: An Old English Christmas Carol.** Putnam's Sons, 1981.

Goudge, Elizabeth. **I Saw Three Ships.** Illustrated by Margot Tomes. Coward, McCann, and Geoghegan, 1969.

Kent, Jack. **Jack Kent's Twelve Days of Christmas.** Scholastic Books, 1973.

Sawyer, Ruth. **Joy to the World.** Illustrated by Trina Hyman. Little, Brown, & Co., 1966.

FOLK SONGS

Aliki. **Go Tell Aunt Rhody.** Macmillan, 1974.

Aliki. **Hush Little Baby.** Prentice-Hall, 1974.

Bonne, Rose. **I Know an Old Lady.** Rand McNally, 1961.

Freschet, Bernice. **The Ants Go Marching.** Illustrated by Stefan Martin. Scribner, 1973.

Langstaff, John. **Frog Went A-Courtin!** Illustrated by Feodor Rojankovsky. Harcourt, Brace, Jovanovich, 1955.

Paterson, Andrew B. **Waltzing Matilda.** Holt, Rinehart and Winston, 1972.

Quackenbush, Robert. **Clementine.** Lippincott, 1974.

_____ . **Go Tell Aunt Rhody.** Lippincott, 1973.

_____ . **She'll Be Comin' Round the Mountain.** Lippincott, 1973.

Zemach, Harve. **Mommy, Buy Me a China Doll.** Illustrated by Margot Zemach. Farrar, Straus, and Giroux, 1975.

NURSERY RHYMES

Hale, Sara Josepha. **Mary Had a Little Lamb.** Illustrated by Tomie De Paola. Holiday House, 1984.

Langstaff, John. **Oh, A-Hunting We Will Go.** Illustrated by Nancy W. Parker. Atheneum, 1974.

PATRIOTIC AND HISTORICAL SONGS

Schackburg, Richard. **Yankee Doodle.** Illustrated by Ed Emberley. Prentice-Hall, 1965.

Spier, Peter. **The Erie Canal.** Doubleday, 1970.

———. **London Bridge Is Falling Down!** Doubleday, 1976.

———. **Star-Spangled Banner.** Doubleday, 1973.

Children's Books Involving Instruments and Sound Effects

Carle, Eric. **I See a Song.** Crowell, 1973.
   A burst of color with no words represents an artist's interpretation of the sounds of music when a musician begins to play his violin. Illustrations change as the mood of the music changes.
   Music and art. Play background music while children draw or paint. Ask them to illustrate the music. Loud explosive music or soft pastoral music might be chosen. (I,SG)
   Select music. Select music suggestive of the illustrations for the book. The illustrations call for a variety of music. Have children select the appropriate music from a variety of recordings and tape the selected music in sequence to accompany the illustrations. Play the taped music as the book is viewed. This project will take some adult guidance, but will have values of exposing children to a variety of music and use of real audio equipment. (I,SG,LG)

   Programming notes: Plan to use this title during February, which is National Music Month, or prior to visiting a band or orchestra rehearsal.

Emberley, Barbara. **Drummer Hoff.** Illustrated by Ed Emberley. Prentice-Hall, 1967. Caldecott Medal Award.
   A cumulative story of the preparation and firing of a cannon. Private Parriage brings the carriage as other military personnel collect the barrel, powder, rammer, and shot. General Border gives the order and Drummer Hoff fires the cannon off.
   Drums and other musical instruments. Use drums to beat the rhythm. Use a different drum or cymbals to sound the bang of the firing of the gun. Represent each character and sound with an instrument. Play the instrument each time the character it represents is mentioned. (SG,LG)

Hazen, Barbara. **The Sorcerer's Apprentice.** Illustrated by Tomi Ungerer. Lancelot, 1969.
   A humorous retelling of the story. Illustrations depict the Sorcerer's magic.
   Background music. Use Dukas's music such as recorded on the Columbia label by the New York Philharmonic. Play the music softly as background music as the story is told or read. (LG)
   Flannel board story. Make flannel board characters. Use the background music as suggested above. Play the music as the story is told using the flannel board characters. (SG,LG)

Isadora, Rachel. **Ben's Trumpet.** Greenwillow, 1979. Caldecott Honor Book.
   Ben's friends make fun of him because of his fascination with the sound of a trumpet played by nightclub entertainers in his neighborhood. Ben pretends to play a trumpet and his wish to have one comes true.
   Trumpet player. Invite a trumpet player to demonstrate his talent for the children, or visit a music store or school band to see and hear the trumpets and other instruments played. Be sure to make arrangements for a demonstration of trumpet playing. (LG)

54 / LET'S MAKE MUSIC

Prokofiev, Sergei. **Peter and the Wolf.** Illustrated by Jörg Müller. Knopf, 1986.
    A retelling of the orchestral fairy tale in which Peter ignores his grandfather's warnings and proceeds to capture a wolf. The illustrations set the stage for this tale by showing the instruments that represent each character—the bird by the flute, the duck by the oboe, the cat by the clarinet, the grandfather by the bassoon, the wolf by three French horns, Peter by all the strings of the orchestra, and the gunshots by the drums. The story is illustrated with several beautiful picture frames on a page. A book that children who like the story will want to go back to over and over. Note: This book is available with a narrated audiocassette with music by the Hamburg Symphony Orchestra.
    Listen. Secure a recording of *Peter and the Wolf.* Listen to the recording. Talk about the music, the different sounds and moods. Have the book available for children to go back to. (I,SG,LG)

Schaaf, Peter. **The Violin Close Up.** Four Winds, 1980.
    Close-up photographs show each part of the violin.
    Violin music. Select and listen to recordings of violin music. (I,SG,LG)
    Violinist. Invite a violinist to visit the group. Encourage him or her to tell children about how he or she became interested in playing the violin and to demonstrate playing the violin. (SG,LG)
    Orchestra concert. Attend an orchestra concert or rehearsal. (SG,LG)

    Programming notes: If a child in the group is taking violin lessons, invite him or her to bring in the violin and play for the group. Use this title along with Sergei Prokofiev's *Peter and the Wolf.* Peter is represented by the strings of the orchestra in this production.

Sendak, Maurice. **Maurice Sendak's Really Rosie.** Music by Carole King. Harper & Row, 1975.
    Includes the Nutshell Library stories: "One Was Johnny," "Alligators All Around," "Pierre," and "Chicken Soup and Rice." Rosie is the director, producer, and star of the show. The other actors are the Nutshell Kids. Written in script form, each story is a presentation within the play. Music and words to the songs are included. (LG)
    View film. View the 16 millimeter film *Really Rosie.* Children may need or wish to view the film several times. (SG,LG)
    Act out the story. Select parts of the story to act out. For younger school-age children the complete story would be too involved. However, one child could play Rosie, with costume and all. The Nutshell Library stories are easy to remember—"Alligators All Around" is about the alphabet; "Chicken Soup and Rice," months of the year; and "One Was Johnny," numbers one to ten. (SG)
    Choral reading. "Pierre," the fourth story, has a moral. Pierre, who would only say "I don't care," finds that he should "care." Present "Pierre" in choral reading fashion with one child or all children chanting, "I don't care," and in the end, "I do care," for Pierre. (SG,LG)
    Sing the "Really Rosie" songs. Learn and sing the "Really Rosie" songs. Use the songs as part of the play or just for fun. (SG,LG)

    Programming notes: Use these activities to share examples of Maurice Sendak's work. Spend several days with Maurice Sendak and his works.

Spier, Peter. **Crash! Bang! Boom!** Doubleday, 1972.
    Sounds in a child's world are presented in beautifully colored illustrations. Of course, one must imagine the sounds as the illustrations are viewed. Detailed pictures show items that make various noises. The word labeling the sound is printed next to each picture.
    Sound effects. Select musical instruments for crash, bang, and boom sounds. Use appropriately to accompany the reading of the book. Use the sound in place of the word. For example, use cymbals for crash, slapsticks or sand blocks for bang, and a drum for boom. (SG,LG)

Using Music as an Extension of Children's Picture Book Stories

Anderson, Joan. **Pioneer Children of Appalachia.** Photographs by George Ancona. Clarion, 1986.
   Photographs from Fort New Salem, a living history museum in West Virginia, recreate the pioneer life of young people in Appalachia in the early nineteenth century. They sing such songs as "Froggie Went A-Courtin' " and "Barbara Allen."
   Appalachian music. Find and sing songs mentioned in the title plus other appropriate songs of early America. Listen to a recording of Aaron Copland's "Appalachian Spring." (SG,LG)

Crews, Donald. **Carousel.** Greenwillow, 1982.
   A carousel is illustrated from the time it is empty to the action of riders mounting the horses, the blur of the carousel in motion, back to stopping again. The book contains few words but illustrations filled with action.
   Carousel music. Select music as played by the calliope as a carousel is in operation. Use the music to accompany the viewing of the book. (I,SG,LG)

Feelings, Muriel. **Moja Means One.** Illustrated by Tom Feelings. Dial, 1971. Caldecott Honor Book.
   A Swahili counting book with realistic illustrations. East African culture is depicted in this unusual counting book. Swahili words and pronunciations are given. Depicts aspects of the geography, animals, clothing, musical instruments, children, and mothers.
   African music. Listen to African music. Identify distinctives of the music. What instruments are used? (I,SG,LG)
   African musical instruments. Make African musical instruments to accompany recordings of African music or to make your own music, African style. Suggested instruments include a drum, guitar, jangles, and shakers. (I,SG,LG)
   Drum. Use an oatmeal box or coffee can. Decorate the sides. Retain the lids for a simple drum. More sophisticated drums are made by using the same box or can and lacing flexible material like inner tubing over the ends, lacing from top to bottom to make the drum skin tight.
   Guitar. Use a shoe box or cigar box. Cut a hole in the top lid (about 3 by 3 inches). Decorate the box as desired. Wrap several rubber bands around the box lengthwise so they stretch over the hole. Strum the rubber bands to make music.
   Jangles. For each jangle use a stick or dowel about 8 by ½ inches. Flatten pop bottle caps with a hammer. Attach two bottle caps, with a nail, to each stick. Paint or decorate the stick, if desired.[1]
   Shakers. Secure dried gourds. Dried seeds inside provide the sound when shaken. Decorate as desired with paint, or glue on designs. *Or* use an empty container (powdered drink can with lid, Band-Aid box, plastic detergent bottle with lid). Add pebbles, dried beans, or rice. Decorate as desired.
   Special drum activity. Observe and try out a variety of drums. Again, trips to the music equipment store or the school band room are good sources. (SG,LG)
   Secret codes. Use homemade drum or available commercial drum. Make up codes with drumbeats and send messages. (I,SG)
   Drumbeat patterns. Use drumbeat patterns for names. For example, Ann = X (one beat), Sally = XX (two beats). Chant the names with the drumbeats. Then beat the name without the chant and have children guess the name. (I,SG,LG)

   Additional African titles:

Aardema, Verna. *Bringing the Rain to Kapiti Plain.* Illustrated by Beatriz Vidal. Dial, 1981.

_____ . *Why Mosquitoes Buzz in People's Ears.* Illustrated by Leo Dillon and Diane Dillon. Dial, 1975. Caldecott Medal Book.

McDermott, Gerald. *Anansi the Spider: A Tale from the Ashanti.* Holt, Rinehart and Winston, 1972.

Musgrove, Margaret. *Ashanti to Zulu.* Illustrated by Leo and Diane Dillion. Dial, 1976. Caldecott Medal Award.

Goffstein, M. B. **A Little Schubert.** Harper & Row, 1972.
    A brief biography of Franz Schubert written for young children. Illustrations are line drawings. Included with the book is Peter Schaaf's lyrical recording of five Schubert waltzes.
    Music by Schubert. Follow-up the reading of the story of Schubert by listening to a variety of his music. Check the public library for recordings. (I,SG,LG)

Hutchins, Pat. **Rosie's Walk.** Macmillan, 1968.
    A book of few words about a hen narrowly escaping the fox in the barnyard. The reader sees the fox but it is obvious that the hen does not. The illustrations convey the action of the story.
    Walking music. Select music appropriate to turning the pages of the book depicting Rosie's walk around the barnyard. Instrumental recordings of "Dixie," "Turkey in the Straw," or similar tunes are appropriate. (SG,LG)

Isadora, Rachel. **Opening Night.** Greenwillow, 1984.
    Heather, a young ballerina, experiences the offstage and onstage excitement of opening night at the ballet.
    Ballet. Attend a ballet production or visit a ballet rehearsal. Arrange for a backstage tour, if possible. Have ballet dancer or dancers talk to the children about what they do. Identify the type of music used to accompany ballet dancing. (SG)

    Additional ballet titles:

Isadora, Rachel. *My Ballet Class.* Greenwillow, 1980.

Thomas, William E. *So You Want to Be a Dancer.* Photographs by Ray Bengston and Machal Elam. Julian Messner, 1979.

Keats, Ezra Jack. **Psst! Doggie.** Watts, 1973.
    A cat and a dog wordlessly dance to music of foreign lands.
    Foreign music. Select music appropriate as background music while showing or "reading" the pictures of the book. Listen to music native to several countries. Try Russian or Czechoslovakian polka music. (I,SG,LG)

Keats, Ezra Jack. **Whistle for Willie.** Viking, 1964.
    Learning to whistle for the first time can be hard. A story about a boy who learns to whistle, and then cannot hide from his dog, Willie. His whistle lets Willie know where he is every time.
    Whistle. Practice whistling familiar tunes. Take turns whistling a tune and then have classmates guess the tune. (I,SG,LG)
    Note: The teacher may need to demonstrate and provide some ideas. Humming the tune first helps. Most children learn to whistle around age four. Some never learn to whistle, which is all right.

Martin, Bill, Jr., and John Archambault. **Barn Dance!** Illustrated by Ted Rand. Holt, Rinehart and Winston, 1986.
    A young boy is awakened in the middle of the night. When he goes to the barn, he finds the scarecrow playing the fiddle and the animals enjoying a barn dance. The illustrations capture the rhythm and excitement of an old-fashioned barn dance.

Square dance. Select square dance music. Learn and participate in simple square dancing. Note: Observe a square dance or have a couple demonstrate square dancing and instruct children in simple square dancing routines. Often senior citizens are in square dance groups and would be good resource persons for this demonstration. (SG,LG)

Fiddle player. Invite a fiddle player to visit. Have him play square dance music for the children to hear. (SG,LG)

McCloskey, Robert. **Lentil.** Viking, 1940.

A boy can't carry a tune and becomes concerned because he cannot sing. He is happy, however, when he learns to play a harmonica.

Listen to harmonica music. Listen to recorded harmonica music. Play a harmonica or have a harmonica player visit the group. If available, provide harmonicas for children to play. (I,SG,LG)

Comb harmonica. Make your own harmonica with a comb covered with waxed paper. Cut waxed paper the size to cover both sides of the comb. Hold the paper taut against the comb. Place against lips slightly apart and hum a tune. The sound resembles that of a harmonica. (I,SG)

Peppe, Rodney. **The House That Jack Built.** Delacorte, 1985.

A cumulative story of the house that Jack built. The rhyme begins with "this is the house that Jack built" and continues with many items and characters in Jack's house. For example: "this is the malt ..., this is the rat that ate the malt ..., this is the cat that chased the rat that ate the malt ...," etc.

Instruments. Use different instruments to represent the different characters. Each time the character is mentioned play the instrument assigned to that character. (SG)

Perrault, Charles. **Cinderella.** Illustrated by Marcia Brown. Scribner, 1954. Caldecott Medal Award.

Flowing line drawings and soft colors capture the mood of this traditional fairy tale. Cinderella attends the ball, unrecognized by her stepsisters. She is selected by the Prince to dance with him at the ball. The flowing illustrations depict the waltzing at the ball.

Creative movement. Listen to waltz music or other music that suggests soft, flowing movement. Move creatively to the music. Use scarves to encourage such movement.[2] (I,SG,LG)

Sendak, Maurice. **Where the Wild Things Are.** Harper & Row, 1963.

A story of Max and his encounters with the wild things when he is sent to bed without supper. One activity with the monsters is a wild rumpus.

Wild rumpus music. Select the wildest, loudest music possible for the wild rumpus. Listen to a variety or recordings to find the wildest music. Use the music in connection with creative dramatic and art activities. Consult other chapters for activities to extend experiences with this title. (SG,LG)

Spier, Peter. **Peter Spier's Rain.** Doubleday, 1982.

A wordless book depicting a rainy day in detailed illustrations.

Rain music. Select music that sounds like rain or make your own music using triangles and other instruments that sound like rain. (I,SG,LG)

Rain rhythms. On a rainy day, listen to the rain. What rhythms and sounds does the rain make? (I,SG,LG)

Spier, Peter. **Star-Spangled Banner.** Doubleday, 1973.

Patriotic illustrations depict the text of the song.

Flag parade. Using red, white, and blue streamers and/or flags, march to patriotic or marching music such as "Stars and Stripes Forever." (SG,LG)

Stecher, Miriam, and Alice Kandell. **Max, the Music Maker.** Illustrated by Alice S. Kandell. Lothrop, Lee and Shepard, 1980.

Max learns that there is music in everyday sounds.

Everyday sounds. Listen and record everyday sounds. Select music to correspond or duplicate sounds. For example: The ocean or sea, listen to *Sea Gulls* by Hap Palmer; horses clopping, the "Grand Canyon Suite." (I,SG,LG)

Wildsmith, Brian. **Brian Wildsmith's Circus.** Watts, 1970.

Beautiful pictures of the circus depicting colors, action, and movement of the circus people and animals.

Circus music. Select circus music to use while showing the pictures of this book. Use the music for background for a circus parade. (SG,LG)

Programming notes: Use this title and music activity before or after a visit to the circus.

NOTES

[1]Michele Borba and Dan Ungaro, *Bookends* (Carthage, Ill.: Good Apple, 1982), 105.

[2]Linda Leonard Lamme, *Learning to Love Literature: Preschool Through Grade 3* (Urbana, Ill.: National Council of Teachers of English, 1981), 62.

5
LET'S COOK
Children's Literature and Cooking Experiences

School-age children love to cook. They get real satisfaction and enjoyment from the cooking process as well as the finished product. Cooking projects as an extension of their literature provide new experiences and give children opportunity to relate children's literature to real aspects of their lives. Through cooking experiences, children use initiative, develop competence, use real tools, and continue the development of self-help skills.

Cooking experiences give children opportunities to choose recipes, make shopping lists for ingredients, and actually shop for the groceries needed to complete the recipe. Cooking activities give children the opportunity to assist in their own snack preparation and special occasion meals. Older school-age children with a real interest in cooking can be encouraged to collect their own recipes in a book or on file cards. Of course, trying out selected recipes is part of the fun. Cooking activities can be done by individual children or with a small group. The finished product, of course, can be enjoyed by the entire group.

VALUES OF USING LITERATURE BASED COOKING EXPERIENCES

- To provide real life experiences that children can participate in, using real tools and materials.

- To give children some firsthand technical skills as well as a feeling of power and competence.

- To provide learning experiences in the area of sensory awareness—visual, smelling, and tasting.

- To give children opportunities in science to watch changes that occur to ingredients as they cook.

- To provide opportunity to teach children about nutrition.

- To provide firsthand experiences with math/science concepts such as measuring, one-to-one relationships, sequence, and temperature.

- To provide reinforcement of reading and following direction skills by using recipes.

- To provide opportunities for practicing of money management and calculation skills necessary for buying groceries.

- To provide children with satisfying social experiences of cooperation and a sense of belonging and contributing to a group.

- To provide opportunities for achievement, enjoyment, and satisfaction.

60 / LET'S COOK

TECHNIQUES FOR COOKING ACTIVITIES

- Select recipes that are simple enough for the children to handle most of the steps themselves.
- Select foods that are nourishing, such as whole grain flour, fruits, and vegetables.
- Use limited amounts of refined sugar.
- Prepare a graphic recipe on poster board or flip chart for children to follow.
- Use good health and cleanliness techniques of washing hands and cleaning up after preparation.
- Provide a cooking center with cooking utensils and equipment.
- Supervise activities carefully when equipment with potential danger is used.
- Be ready—collect utensils and ingredients ahead of time.

METHODS OF EVALUATION

- Observe for an increased interest and requests for books and materials on foods.
- Observe children's interest, participation, and requests for repeated or similar activities.
- Ask such questions as: Was the activity a satisfying experience? Did the recipe work? Was the activity too hard or too easy for the children?

CHILDREN'S LITERATURE AND COOKING EXPERIENCES

Aleichem, Sholom. **Hanukah Money.** Illustrated by Uri Shulevitz. Greenwillow, 1978.
   A story of the Hanukkah celebration including the traditional lighting of the Hanukkah candles, frying potato pancakes, and the holiday custom of giving money to children during this season of celebration.
   Potato pancakes. Make potato latkes or pancakes, traditionally served during Hanukkah. (SG)

Hanukkah Potato Pancakes

4 large potatoes, grated and drained	2 tablespoons all-purpose flour
4 tablespoons grated onion	1 egg
½ teaspoon salt	2 tablespoons butter
¼ teaspoon pepper	

   Beat egg. Add potatoes, onion, salt, pepper, and flour. Melt butter in frying pan. Drop potato mixture in frying pan using a large serving spoon. Fry until brown on both sides. Serve while hot. Use sour cream or applesauce as topping. Note: For children, the onion may be omitted or reduced to 1 tablespoon.

Aliki. **Corn Is Maize: The Gift of the Indians.** Crowell, 1976.
   A story of how corn grows, how it was discovered, and how it is harvested and processed.
   Corn bread. Use a corn muffin or corn bread mix or use the following recipe.

Golden Corn Bread

1 cup yellow cornmeal	¼ cup shortening, soft
1 cup sifted all-purpose flour	4 teaspoons baking powder
¼ cup sugar	½ teaspoon salt
1 cup milk	1 egg

Sift together cornmeal, flour, sugar, baking powder, and salt in a bowl. Add egg, milk, and shortening. Beat with a rotary beater until smooth, about 1 minute. Bake in greased 8-inch square baking pan in preheated hot oven at 425 degrees Fahrenheit for 20-25 minutes. (I,SG)

Indian Bread

2 cups cornmeal	2 teaspoons baking powder
dash of salt	milk (enough to make the batter stiff)

Make into round patties. Fry in deep fat in an electric skillet and serve hot with butter. (I,SG)

Programming notes: Use these cooking activities with an American Indian theme.

Asch, Frank. **Good Lemonade.** Illustrated by Marie Zimmerman. Watts, 1976.

A young boy had trouble selling his lemonade until he made good lemonade. Good lemonade is always a sure sale on a hot day.

Lemonade

1 lemon	1 cup water
2 tablespoons sugar	ice

Cut the lemon in half. Squeeze 2 tablespoons lemon juice. Put in glass. Add the sugar and stir well. Pour the water into the glass and stir. Serve with ice. Do the same for each glass or multiply the ingredients by the number of servings needed.

Lemonade stand. Set up a lemonade stand. Make signs. Decide on price. Decide on needs and job assignments. Sell lemonade with token coins or real money. (SG)

Programming notes: An especially good summer activity. A small group of children can have experiences with planning, calculating, and real work as they have the lemonade stand.

Bemelmans, Ludwig. **Madeline.** Viking, 1939. Caldecott Honor Book.

_____ . **Madeline's Rescue.** Viking, 1953. Caldecott Medal Award.

Adventures of Madeline and the friends of her boarding school in Paris.

French Toast

slices of bread	4 eggs
1 cup milk	½ teaspoon vanilla extract
½ teaspoon cinnamon	

Beat eggs and other ingredients together. Dip the bread in the egg mixture, then brown both sides in a well-buttered skillet over medium heat. Top with maple syrup, honey, or fresh fruit and sour cream. (I,SG)

62 / LET'S COOK

Programming notes: French toast makes a good morning snack.

Brown, Marcia. **Stone Soup.** Scribner, 1947. Caldecott Honor Book.
   An old tale of three hungry soldiers who tricked weary peasants into giving them the things they needed for soup after they threatened to make soup from stones.
   Stone soup. Everybody's contribution is important. The soup gets better as each person adds his contribution. Select a soup stone, wash and add to pot. Additional ingredients: Prepare and add potatoes, barley, carrots, beef bones, salt, pepper, celery, tomatoes or tomato juice, and some water. Cook slowly for several hours. Enjoy soup together. (SG,LG)

Vegetable Soup

12 potatoes, peeled and chopped
8 carrots, peeled and chopped
3 onions, peeled and chopped
4 celery stalks, peeled and chopped
1 large soup bone and stew meat cut in small pieces
12 ears of corns, cut corn from cob
3 cans tomatoes
1 can baby limas

   Place the bone and stew meat in a large kettle. Cover with water. Boil until the meat is tender. Add all the raw vegetables. Cook the stew until the vegetables are done. Add the canned vegetables. Simmer over low heat. Season with salt and pepper to taste. Serve hot. The soup can be made one day, refrigerated, heated back up, and served the next. Note: Vegetables can be precooked before soup day.

Programming notes: Use soup for lunch or afternoon snack. This recipe is also good for Thanksgiving. Have children contribute ingredients for the soup.

Bunting, Eve. **St. Patrick's Day in the Morning.** Illustrated by Jan Brett. Houghton-Mifflin, 1980.
   The adventures of Jamie, who proves he is not too young to march in the St. Patrick's Day parade. Irish countryside and characters are illustrated. Children easily relate to the excitement of celebrating this holiday.

Shamrock or Butter Cookies

1 cup (2 sticks) butter
1 cup sugar
1 egg
1 tablespoon milk

2¾ cups all-purpose flour
1 teaspoon baking powder
¼ teaspoon salt
1 teaspoon vanilla extract

   Mix all ingredients above. Chill for ease in handling. Roll onto sheet 1/8 inch thick. Cut with shamrock shaped cookie cutters. Place on baking sheet. Sprinkle with green decorator sugar. Bake 350 degrees Fahrenheit for 8 to 10 minutes. (SG)

Carle, Eric. **The Honeybee and the Robber.** Philomel, 1981.
   Adventures of a honeybee including gathering the nectar to filling the beeswax with honey. The bee stings the nose of the bear, "the robber," to protect the beehive. A book with movable parts that might be too fragile for children younger than school-age. Beautiful illustrations. In the back of the book factual information about bees, which is valuable for teachers and children, is given about each page.
   Taste honey. Have honey for snack. Serve on biscuits or buttered toast. (I,SG,LG)
   Honey balls. Make honey balls for snack.

Children's Literature and Cooking Experiences / 63

Honey Balls

1 cup peanut butter
5 tablespoons nonfat dry milk
¼ cup raisins
¼ cup honey
½ cup coconut

Mix above ingredients. Form into balls. Roll in powdered sugar or sesame seeds, if desired. Makes sixteen honey balls. (I,SG)

Programming notes: Use this title independently, with a theme about honeybees, or as an example of Carle's illustration technique. A variety of activities in art, music, and cooking can be planned as extensions of Carle's children's books. Plan an Eric Carle day. Display and share a variety of his books. Give children a choice of the follow-up activities they would like to participate in. Allow time for sharing.

Carle, Eric. **The Secret Birthday Message.** Crowell, 1972.
An unusual book using a code to express a birthday message. Basic shapes are used as a code to correspond to letters in the "Happy Birthday Message."

Giant Birthday Cookies

1 roll (17 ounces) refrigerated sugar cookies
Desired flavor of ready-to-spread frosting in cans
Decorator frosting and pastry tube

Line large cookie sheet with foil, extending foil over edges. Cut well-chilled dough into thirty-six (¼ inch) slices. Arrange eleven slices, sides touching in a circle on foil lined cookie sheet. Use seven slices to fill in circle. (It may be necessary to cut a few slices in half to fill in circle.) Repeat steps with remaining slices. Bake at 350 degrees for 12 to 15 minutes or until puffy and golden brown. Cool completely in pan on cooling rack. Carefully peel foil from back of cookie. Place cookie on serving plate or tray. Frost and decorate as desired. Cut into wedges. (SG)

Programming notes: This is an easy, fast way for a small group of children to make a different birthday dessert. Be sure to have children write happy birthday in the secret code.

Cavognaro, David, and Maggie Cavognaro. **The Pumpkin People.** Sierra Club Books, 1979.
A boy and his father share their pumpkin harvest with their neighbors.
Toasted pumpkin seeds. Wash the seeds from the pumpkin and let dry. Place on a baking sheet and bake for 10 minutes at 325 degrees. Take out of the oven and salt lightly. Let cool and then enjoy eating them. (SG,LG)

Pumpkin Cookies

½ cup (1 stick) butter
¾ cup honey
1 egg
1 teaspoon vanilla extract
1 cup cooked or canned pumpkin
2½ cups all-purpose flour
1 teaspoon baking powder
1 teaspoon baking soda
1 teaspoon nutmeg
1 teaspoon cinnamon

Mix first five ingredients. Sift together dry ingredients and add to wet ingredients. Drop by teaspoon onto a greased cookie sheet. Bake for 15 minutes at 350 degrees. When the cookies come out of the oven make faces on them with raisins. (SG)

64 / LET'S COOK

Programming notes: Use these recipes at Halloween. Save the seeds and pumpkin from the cut out eyes, nose, and mouth of the jack-o'-lantern for the cooking activities. A small group of children might be responsible for making the cookie dough, but each child should be allowed to decorate his or her own pumpkin cookie.

Clark, Margery. **Poppy Seed Cakes.** Illustrated by Maud and Miska Petersham. Doubleday, 1924.

Two Russian born immigrants become friends and share many good times together when they become neighbors in New York City. They enjoy eating together their traditional poppy seed cakes.

Poppy Seed Cake or Bread

- 3 cups all-purpose flour
- 2 cups sugar
- 3 eggs
- 1½ teaspoons baking powder
- 1½ teaspoons salt
- 1½ teaspoons poppy seeds
- 1½ cups milk
- ¾ cup vegetable oil
- 1½ teaspoons vanilla extract
- 1½ teaspoons almond extract
- 1½ teaspoons butter flavoring

Combine all ingredients in a large bowl; beat 2 minutes at medium speed of electric mixer. Spoon batter into two greased and floured 8-by-4-by-3-inch loaf pans. Bake at 350 degrees for 1 hour or until a wooden toothpick inserted in the center comes out clean. Cool loaves in pans 10 minutes. Remove from pans and cool completely on wire racks. Drizzle bread with orange glaze. Makes two loaves.

Orange Glaze

- 1 cup sifted powdered sugar
- ¼ teaspoon vanilla extract
- ¼ teaspoon butter flavoring
- 2 tablespoons orange juice
- ¼ teaspoon almond extract

Combine and mix well. (SG)

Programming notes: Make poppy seed cakes to go along with the stone soup.

Credle, Ellis. **Down, Down the Mountain.** Nelson, c1934, 1961.

A story of Hetty and Hank, children who lived in the Blue Ridge Mountains. They wanted some shoes for winter more than anything but could not afford them. Their grandmother suggested that they plant turnips to sell. They raised a good crop of turnips, harvested them, and went down the mountain to sell them. As they went down the mountain, they gave all but one turnip away. With no turnips to sell they entered this turnip in the fair and to their surprise won first place and enough money to buy shoes. See Janina Domanska's *The Turnip* for recipes.

D'Aulaire, Ingri, and Edgar P. D'Aulaire. **George Washington.** Doubleday, 1936.

The story of George Washington from boyhood to president. The childhood story about when he told his father that he was the one who chopped down the cherry tree is included.

Cherry tarts. Use prepared cherry pie filling and tart shells. Spoon pie filling into tart shells. Top with a spoon of whipped topping. Note: Cherry tarts, pie, or cobbler can also be made from fresh cherries. Check your favorite cookbook for recipes. (SG)

Programming notes: Serve cherry tarts after sharing the George Washington story on his birthday. Ready-baked tart shells and canned cherry pie filling will allow each child to make his or her own tart.

De Paola, Tomie. **Pancakes for Breakfast.** Harcourt, Brace, Jovanovich, 1978.
   A humorous story of how a woman gets ingredients for pancakes for breakfast.
   Pancakes. Make pancakes. Use a mix that requires eggs and milk. Have butter and maple syrup to go with pancakes. (SG,LG)

De Paola, Tomie. **The Popcorn Book.** Holiday House, 1978.
   A story about popcorn based on factual information. Two recipes are included in the book. Stories and legends about popcorn are told using humorous illustrations.
   Popcorn. Use the recipes in the book. (SG,LG)

De Paola, Tomie. **Strega Nona.** Prentice-Hall, 1975. Caldecott Honor Book.
   An old tale of a magic pasta pot and the dilemma of a young boy in the employ of Strega Nona when he decides to feed the village pasta but does not know how to stop the pot from producing. Strega Nona, the witch, knows the magic spell.
   Pasta. Cook pasta (spaghetti) for snack. Follow package directions. Add spaghetti sauce, tomato sauce, and/or cheese before eating. (SG,LG)

   Programming notes: Tomie De Paola has several titles with food as the subject. Present these titles and a choice of cooking activities or use each title and cooking experience independently.

De Regniers, Beatrice Schenk. **May I Bring a Friend?** Illustrated by Beni Montresor. Atheneum, 1964.
   The king invites a boy to visit him. Each day of the week he is invited for a different event—tea, dinner, lunch, breakfast, Halloween, and Apple Pie Day. Each day the boy brings a different friend from the zoo and on Saturday he invites the king and queen to the zoo to have tea with all his animal friends.
   Snack for each day. Have children plan a snack for each day of the week. Here are some suggestions.
   Monday—Tea cakes or sugar cookies and spiced apple juice. Use refrigerator sugar cookies. Slice and bake as directed on the package. For spiced apple juice, heat apple juice with 3 or 4 cinnamon sticks. Serve warm. (SG,LG)
   Tuesday—Fruit kebabs. Have a variety of fruits such as bananas, apples, pears, strawberries, and grapes. Prepare bananas, apples, and pears in slices or wedges. Make kebabs by placing a choice of fruits on large toothpicks or plastic skewers. (SG,LG)
   Wednesday—Individual pizzas.

   8 English muffins, cut in half
   1 8-ounce can pizza topping
   2 teaspoons minced onion
   1 cup shredded mozzarella cheese
   Sliced pepperoni, olives, mushrooms

   Place muffin halves on cookie sheet. Spread with pizza topping mix. Add pepperoni or other choice of ingredients. Sprinkle with grated cheese. Bake at 450 degrees for 10 to 15 minutes. (I,SG,LG)

   Thursday—Vegetables and dip. See Ellis Credle's *Down, Down the Mountain* and Janina Domanska's *The Turnip* in this chapter for vegetable suggestions and dip recipe. (SG,LG)
   Friday—Apple pie. The following recipe makes a quick and easy apple pie.

66 / LET'S COOK

Apple Cobbler

1 tablespoon butter, melted
1 cup flour
1 cup milk
2 teaspoons baking powder
¼ teaspoon salt
1 can apple pie filling

Melt the butter. Pour it in the bottom of a casserole dish. Mix the flour, milk, baking powder, and salt. Pour the mixture over the butter. Pour the pie filling on top. Bake at 350 degrees for 45 minutes. (SG,LG)

Devlin, Wende, and Harry Devlin. **Cranberry Thanksgiving.** Parent's Magazine Press, 1971.
Maggie invites a special guest to Thanksgiving dinner. One of the special treats is grandmother's cranberry bread.
Cranberry bread. Make cranberry bread. Follow the recipe in the back of the book or use cranberry bread mix. (SG)

Cranberry Relish

4 cups cranberries
2 apples
2 oranges (seedless)
1¾ cups sugar

Wash cranberries, apples, and oranges. Cut apples in quarters. Take out core and cut oranges in quarters. Put cranberries, oranges, and apples in food processor. Add sugar to ground fruits and mix well. Fill in clean baby food jars and store in refrigerator. (SG)

Programming notes: Use in connection with the Thanksgiving theme. What Thanksgiving is complete without cranberries?

Domanska, Janina. **The Turnip.** Macmillan, 1969.
A delightful retelling of a classic, cumulative tale. Grandfather planted the turnip and grandmother watered it daily. When it was ready to harvest, they needed help to pull it out of the ground. The illustrations help the tale build simply and rhythmically to a funny climax and ending.
Taste turnips. Turnips are not a widely used vegetable. They have a distinct taste that one either likes or dislikes. Many children may never have tasted a turnip. Turnips may be eaten raw or cooked. (I,SG,LG)
Raw turnips. Peel turnips and cut into strips. Use with other fresh vegetables (carrots, broccoli, cauliflower, cucumbers) for a snack. Use a dip such as the following to make eating the vegetables more appealing. (I,SG,LG)

Yummy Dip

1 cup sour cream
4-6 slices bacon, cooked crisp and crumbled
½ cup chili sauce

Mix all ingredients. Chill. Serve with chips or raw vegetables.

Cooked turnips. Serve cooked turnips with corn bread and other vegetables. (SG,LG)

Turnips

1 pound turnips
½ teaspoon salt
½ teaspoon sugar
1 tablespoon butter

Peel and slice turnips. Place sliced turnips in a saucepan. Add just enough water to cover the turnips. Add salt and sugar. Bring to a boil and cook 10 to 15 minutes, or until tender. Drain, place in a serving dish, add butter, and serve. Note: Tender turnip tops may be washed and cooked as greens.

Programming notes: Use these titles along with Cynthia Rylant's *When I Was Young in the Mountains.* Also, consider the following activities:

- Plan a visit in the fall to a farm or a produce market to secure the turnips and other vegetables harvested in the fall.

- Visit the county fair. Be sure to visit the fair booths to see the turnips and other vegetables entered in the judging competition. Make note of the winners, especially first place winners.

Gage, Wilson. **Squash Pie.** Illustrated by Glen Rounds. Morrow, 1976.

A humorous story about a farmer who plants squash because he wants squash pie; unfortunately, something keeps stealing his squash. The squash pie his wife serves him is very humorous. What does real squash pie taste like?

Squash pie. Substitute cooked, drained, and mashed squash for pumpkin. Use your favorite pumpkin pie recipe. (SG)

The Gingerbread Boy. Retold and illustrated by Paul Galdone. Seabury Press, 1975.

The little woman made the gingerbread boy who jumped off the baking pan and ran away. The traditional folk tale boldly illustrated.

Gingerbread men. Make gingerbread men. Allow children to decorate with raisins, cinnamon candy, and frosting. (SG,LG)

Gingerbread Cookies

1 cup shortening
1 cup brown sugar
3 eggs
2 cups molasses
2 tablespoons cinnamon
8 cups all-purpose flour
2 teaspoons soda
1 teaspoon salt
2 teaspoons ginger

Preheat oven to 375 degrees. In a bowl, cream sugar and shortening. Add eggs and molasses. Mix. Sift dry ingredients over waxed paper. Add to mixture and stir well. Put in refrigerator until cold. Roll out on cutting board to ½ inch thick. Cut out with gingerbread boy cookie cutter. Stick raisins on for eyes and buttons. Bake 8 to 10 minutes.[1]

Programming notes: Making gingerbread men is a perfect follow up for the Gingerbread Man story. Gingerbread men can also be made at Christmas. Gingerbread dough can be made ahead and each child can then have the experience of rolling, cutting, and decorating his or her own gingerbread man.

Hoban, Lillian. **Arthur's Christmas Cookies.** Harper & Row, 1972.

Arthur, a chimpanzee, has no money for presents so he decides to make cookies for his family. He uses salt instead of sugar, so his cookies are different. They cannot be eaten but make perfect new Christmas tree ornaments—presents members of his family can enjoy and keep. While making the ornaments, they have hot chocolate to drink.

68 / LET'S COOK

Christmas party. Serve real sugar cookies and hot chocolate. Use the same Christmas cookie cutters as used for the tree ornaments suggested for this title in the chapter "Let's Celebrate." (A good sugar cookie recipe is found in this chapter for St. Patrick's Day.) Make hot chocolate, using the following recipe. (SG,LG)

Instant Hot Chocolate Mix

2¾ cups instant nonfat dry milk powder
1½ cups instant cocoa mix for milk
½ cup nondairy coffee creamer
½ cup powdered sugar
1 cup miniature marshmallows (optional)

Combine ingredients in a large bowl and mix well. Store hot chocolate mix in an airtight container. To serve, place ⅓ cup mix in a cup. Add 1 cup boiling water and stir well. Makes 5 cups mix or serves 15. Note: Marshmallows or whipped cream may be added to the top of the hot chocolate before serving.

Programming notes: Consult the Christmas section of the "Let's Celebrate" chapter for additional suggestions for *Arthur's Christmas Cookies* and other titles to use at Christmas.

Hoban, Russell. **A Birthday for Frances.** Illustrated by Lillian Hoban. Harper & Row, 1968.
Frances has a difficult time accepting the fact that the family is celebrating her sister Gloria's birthday and that she must wait her turn. But she does in the end.
Birthday cake. Use a cake mix for the cake. Frost with prepared frosting and decorate.
Birthday cake ice cream cones. Fill waffle ice cream cones with cake batter a little over one-half full. Place on cookie sheet and bake like cupcakes. Ice with prepared frosting and decorate. Eat the whole thing.

Hoban, Russell. **Bread and Jam for Frances.** Illustrated by Lillian Hoban. Harper & Row, 1964.
Frances, a badger, refuses to eat anything but bread and jam. She does not want eggs for breakfast cooked in any way—soft boiled, sunny-side-up, scrambled, or poached. Other nutritious meals at home and school are offered to Frances. She refuses to eat anything but bread and jam. Mother serves Frances raspberry, strawberry, and gooseberry jam on biscuits or toast until she gets so tired of bread and jam that she asks for other foods.
Bread and jam. Serve bread and jam. Try a variety of jams. Make toast or bake biscuits. A quick way to make biscuits is to use the commercial biscuit mix following the directions on the package, or use canned biscuits. (SG,LG)
Make breakfast. Fix eggs in all the ways Frances's mother suggests. Try soft boiled, hard boiled, sunny-side-up, scrambled, or poached eggs. Allow children to choose and prepare their choice. (SG,LG)

Programming notes: See John Lord's *The Giant Jam Sandwich* in this chapter for a recipe for strawberry jam.

Hogrogain, Nonny. **Carrot Cake.** Greenwillow, 1977.
A rabbit and his bride had trouble getting along. The story ends with them peacefully eating a carrot cake.
Carrot cake. For convenience, use a carrot cake mix. Bake the cake as directed on the cake mix directions; frost with a choice of icing. Or make a carrot cake using the following recipe. Children will enjoy the process of grating the carrots in preparation for the cake. Caution: If a grater is used children must be informed of safety precautions for using a grater. (SG)

Carrot Cake

4 eggs
2 cups sugar
1½ cups corn oil
3 cups grated raw carrots

2 cups plain all-purpose flour
1 teaspoon cinnamon
1 teaspoon salt
2 teaspoons soda
½ cup pecans, chopped (optional)

Beat eggs and sugar together. Add oil gradually. Sift dry ingredients together. Add carrots and dry ingredients. Mix well. Add pecans. Use greased and floured pans. Place batter in three 8-inch layer pans or one tube pan. Bake in oven at 350 degrees for 20-25 minutes for layers or 325 degrees for 1½ hours for tube pan.

Icing

1 8-ounce package cream cheese
1½ sticks butter

1 teaspoon vanilla extract
1 box powdered sugar, sifted

Have cream cheese and butter at room temperature. Beat cream cheese and butter together until light and fluffy. Blend in sugar and vanilla extract. Add a little milk if needed to make the icing spreadable. Ice cake after it has cooled.

Programming notes: Use this activity with other stories about rabbits such as Leo Lionni's *Let's Make Rabbits.*

Hosea, Tobias, and Lisa Baskin. **Hosea's Alphabet.** Viking, 1972. Caldecott Honor Book.
An alphabet book very appropriate for school-age children. Illustrations are somewhat abstract and the selection for each letter of the alphabet is more difficult than the typical alphabet illustrations.

Alphabet soup. Add alphabet noodles to favorite canned soup. Alphabet noodles show up well in vegetable soup. Select canned soup and prepare by directions on the label.

Additional ABC titles:

Anno, Mitsumasa. *Anno's Alphabet.* Crowell, 1974.

Emberley, Edward R. *Ed Emberley's ABC.* Little, Brown, & Co., 1978.

Fife, Dale. *Adam's ABC.* Little, Brown, & Co., 1971.

Lobel, Arnold. *On Market Street.* Illustrated by Anita Lobel. Greenwillow, 1981.

Sendak, Maurice. *Alligators All Around.* Harper & Row, 1962.

Wildsmith, Brian. *Brian Wildsmith's ABC.* Watts, 1963.

Programming notes: Alphabet soup is fun and a great snack to prepare while looking at alphabet books. The alphabet books listed above are especially appropriate for school-age children. Use alphabet soup when making alphabet books, as suggested as a follow-up activity for *Bruno Munari's ABC* in the "Let's Create" chapter.

Howe, James. **The Day the Teacher Went Bananas.** Illustrated by Lillian Hoban. Dutton, 1984.
A delightfully funny story of a gorilla who came to school as a substitute teacher. The children learned a lot of gorilla tricks and mannerisms to the point of chaos. The principal said that they all belonged in the zoo. The children visited their favorite teacher the next day at the zoo and took bananas for lunch.

Banana snacks. Serve bananas for a snack. Think of different ways to prepare bananas. Use some of the following suggestions.

Banana Sandwich I

Use two slices of bread. Spread one slice with peanut butter. Add sliced bananas. Top with the second slice of bread. (I,SG)

Banana Sandwich II

Peel banana. Slice banana lengthwise. Spread one slice with peanut butter and top with the other slice of banana. (I,SG)

Fried Bananas

Peel banana. Slice banana lengthwise. Heat 1 tablespoon of butter in the bottom of a frying pan over medium to low heat. Brown bananas on both sides. Serve with brown sugar and lemon juice or pancake syrup. (I,SG)

Frozen Bananas

Peel banana. Insert a popsicle stick into banana from one end. Dip banana in chocolate syrup, then roll in pecan pieces. Freeze for two hours before serving. (I,SG)

Banana Milk Shake

Combine 1 banana, sliced, 6 to 8 scoops vanilla ice cream, and 2 cups cold milk in a blender. Blend until smooth. Serves 4. Note: For one serving use ¼ banana, sliced, 2 to 3 scoops vanilla ice cream, and ½ cup cold milk. (I,SG)

Banana Split

For each banana split, slice lengthwise ½ peeled banana. Place in a bowl. Add 1 or 2 scoops of ice cream and toppings. Toppings might include chocolate sprinkles or syrup, fruit toppings, nuts, whipped cream, and maraschino cherries. Note: Using ½ banana makes a smaller banana split. Older children may be able to eat a regular banana split using a whole banana and more ice cream. (I,SG)

Johnny-Cake. Retold by Joseph Jacobs. Illustrated by Emma L. Brock. Putnam's Sons, 1967.

A typical folk tale, an old woman made a johnnycake. When she opened the oven, he rolled away from several different characters, only to be eaten in the end by a fox.

Johnny-cake. Look for a recipe of johnnycakes (cornmeal pancakes) on the back of a package of cornmeal. Serve johnnycakes with syrup and butter.

Langstaff, John. **Hot Cross Buns and Other Old Street Cries.** Illustrated by Nancy Winslow Parker. Atheneum, 1978.

Hot cross buns, an English tradition at Easter time, is included in this collection of old street chants. Especially good for school-age children who love chants.

Hot cross buns. Make or buy hot cross buns from the bakery to serve at snack time. Hot cross buns are yeast buns with currants and candied fruit baked inside. Each has a cross of white icing on the top.

Lexau, Joan. **Striped Ice Cream.** Lippincott, 1968 (also Scholastic, 1971).

Becky, the youngest of five children, was afraid she would not get her favorite striped ice cream for her birthday because her older brothers and sisters needed new shoes. Just as she was sure her whole family had forgotten her birthday, they surprised her with her favorite ice cream.

Striped ice cream. Serve striped or marbleized ice cream such as fudge or raspberry ripple. Ice cream in a cone makes it even more special. (SG,LG)

The Little Red Hen. Illustrated by Paul Galdone. Seabury Press, 1973.

The Little Red Hen could not talk any of her friends into helping make the bread, but they were all ready to eat it.

Bake bread. Make some bread. Yeast bread would be fun. Use a mix to make a loaf of bread. Serve while hot.

Programming notes: Several folk tales like *The Little Red Hen* might be extended with cooking experiences. Make porridge after reading *The Three Bears* or goodies for grandma as a response to *Little Red Riding Hood*. Instant oatmeal makes good porridge. Serve oatmeal topped with jam or brown sugar and butter. Have children plan goodies they would like to make for grandma—cookies, muffins, no-cook candy, etc.

Lord, John Vernon. **The Giant Jam Sandwich.** Houghton-Mifflin, 1973.

Amusing story of the citizens of Itching Down who made a giant jam sandwich to capture the wasps that were bothering them.

Make jam. Make jam for sandwiches (recipe below). Serve plain jam sandwiches. Spread jam on slices of bread. Serve on a single slice of bread for an open-faced sandwich or put two slices together with jam in the middle for a sandwich. Variation: Add peanut butter to the jam sandwich or serve jam on warm buttered toast. (I,SG)

No-Cook Strawberry Jam

1 quart fresh strawberries
4 cups sugar
1 box Sure-Jell fruit pectin
¾ cup water

Remove caps from strawberries. Crush fruit one layer at a time. Measure 2 cups strawberries into a large bowl. Stir sugar into strawberries. Let stand 10 minutes. Mix ¾ cup water and Sure-Jell fruit pectin in small saucepan. Bring to a full boil and boil 1 minute, stirring constantly. At once stir into fruit. Continue stirring 3 minutes. (A few sugar crystals will remain.) Immediately pour mixture into 1- or 2-cup glass or rigid plastic containers, leaving ½-inch space at top. Cover at once with lids. Let stand at room temperature 24 hours. Store jam in freezer, or small amounts may be covered and kept in the refrigerator up to 3 weeks. Note: This recipe and other jam and jelly recipes can be found in the Sure-Jell fruit pectin package.

McCloskey, Robert. **Blueberries for Sal.** Viking, 1948. Caldecott Honor Book.

Two families—a child and her mother and a bear cub and his mother—are picking blueberries. The children end up following the wrong mother for a while.

Fresh blueberries. Buy or pick fresh blueberries. Wash and eat. (I,SG,LG)

Blueberry pancakes or muffins. Use a mix for either. Have syrup or honey and butter to go along with the muffins or pancakes. (SG,LG)

McCully, Emily Arnold. **Picnic.** Harper & Row, 1984.

The youngest member of the mouse family is missing. The search by the family shows how much she is missed. The wordless book shows the joys of a picnic and a family reunion.

Picnic. Plan and carry out a picnic. Discuss appropriate picnic foods. Prepare and pack picnic. Select a picnic site and enjoy a picnic together. Sandwiches, chips, and lemonade are good items for a picnic. What do you like for a picnic? Be creative. (LG)

Programming notes: Plan a picnic as part of the Fourth of July celebration.

72 / LET'S COOK

Nursery Rhymes

Little Boy Blue

Haystacks

1 tablespoon smooth peanut butter
1 3-ounce can chow mein noodles
1 cup roasted peanuts
1 6-ounce package butterscotch morsels

    Melt peanut butter and butterscotch morsels together in a heavy saucepan over low heat. Add noodles and peanuts to mixture, and mix until well coated. Form little clusters on foil and set in refrigerator to harden. Makes twenty-four haystacks. (SG)

Little Miss Muffet

Curds and Whey

    Stir 2 cups whole milk over medium heat until it starts to bubble. Remove from heat. Add 1 tablespoon of vinegar and continue stirring until curds form. Strain off the whey, squeezing out any remains with a spoon. Salt lightly and serve on crackers.[2] (SG)

    Programming notes: Have a nursery rhyme unit. Plan a variety of activities including cooking, creative art, dramatics, and music. Allow children to choose the small group activity they wish to participate in. Plan a time to share experiences.

Potter, Beatrix. **A Treasury of Peter Rabbit and Other Stories.** Avenel, 1979.
    A collection of Peter Rabbit stories including the first story about Peter and his adventures in Mr. McGregor's garden. Mother rabbit went to the bakery to buy brown bread and currant buns while his brothers and sisters gathered blackberries and Peter went on his forbidden adventure. When mother returned, Peter was sent to bed with camomile tea while the others had bread, milk, and blackberries for supper.
    Currant buns. Visit a bakery. Buy currant buns and brown bread. Serve with blackberries or blackberry jam and milk. (SG,LG)

Rylant, Cynthia. **When I Was Young in the Mountains.** Illustrated by Diane Goode. Dutton, 1982. Caldecott Honor Book.
    A young girl recalls her life in the mountains of the rural south. Beautiful illustrations depict mountain life.
    Mountain food. Cook pinto beans, corn bread, and fried okra, or make hot cocoa as mentioned in the story. (SG,LG)

Scheer, Julian. **Rain Makes Applesauce.** Illustrated by Marvin Bileck. Holiday House, 1964. Caldecott Honor Book.
    A repetitive story about things that happen all around. After each statement, rain makes applesauce is repeated.

Applesauce

Six apples   ½ cup sugar
½ cup water   dash of cinnamon

    Peel and core (take the seeds out) six apples. Slice the apples. Cook in water until tender. Drain and mash with a fork. Add the sugar and cinnamon.[3] (SG)

Children's Literature and Cooking Experiences / 73

Programming notes: Making applesauce is a must as part of a fall unit. See "Let's Create" chapter for additional ideas to include in a theme on apples.

Scheer, Julian. **Upside Down Day.** Illustrated by Kelly Oechsli. Holiday House, 1968.

On an upside-down day things do not happen as they usually do. For example, "Bees won't sting" and "Bells won't ring." Many opposites or reverses are included.

Upside-down cake. Make an upside-down cake. Allow the whole group to sample the cake. (SG,LG)

Pineapple Upside-Down Cake

½ cup (1 stick) butter
1 cup packed brown sugar
1 No. 2½ can pineapple rings, drained
Maraschino cherries
1 box yellow cake mix

Melt butter in a 9- or 10-inch skillet over low heat. Add sugar to melted butter in the skillet and mix well. Arrange pineapple rings on butter and sugar mixture. Add a maraschino cherry to the middle of each pineapple ring. Use cake mix to make cake batter. Follow cake mix directions. Pour batter over the butter, sugar, and fruit mixture. Bake at 350 degrees for 30 minutes or until done. Remove from oven and turn upside down on serving plate, leaving the pan over the cake briefly. Remove pan and serve upside down.

Sendak, Maurice. **Chicken Soup with Rice: A Book About Months.** Harper & Row, 1962.

"I told you once/I told you twice/All seasons of the year are nice/for eating chicken soup and rice!" A delightful rhyming verse about the months of the year.

Make chicken soup (canned is convenient) and rice. Add rice to chicken soup. A hearty snack for winter or any season. (SG,LG)

Sendak, Maurice. **Where the Wild Things Are.** Harper & Row, 1963. Caldecott Medal Award.

Max dreams of wild things when he is sent to this room without supper. Illustrations present believable, friendly monsters who enjoy having Max around.

Cookie Monsters

½ cup (1 stick) butter, softened
½ teaspoon lemon flavoring
¼ teaspoon salt

½ cup powdered sugar
1¼ cups all-purpose flour

Cream the butter and sugar in a bowl. Stir in the lemon flavoring. Measure the flour and salt together and pour onto waxed paper. Pick up the waxed paper and shake about half the flour/salt mixture into the bowl containing the butter/sugar mixture. Stir well. Shake the rest of the flour/salt mixture into the bowl. Stir well. Cover the bowl with waxed paper or plastic wrap and put it in the refrigerator to chill. After an hour, take the dough out of the refrigerator. Set the oven for 375 degrees. Pinch off some dough and roll it around in your hands until it gets soft enough to shape. Mold the dough into playful monsters with fun heads, ears, legs, noses, tails, eyes, and tusks. Be creative! Use your imagination. Put the cookie monsters on the cookie sheet as you shape them and leave room for them to spread as they bake. Bake for about 8 to 10 minutes, until golden brown.[4] (SG,LG)

Programming notes: Use the cookie monsters as one of the activities to extend children's experiences with this title. Additional activities are suggested in all the other chapters.

Seuss, Dr. **Green Eggs and Ham.** Random House, 1960.

The main character says he does not like green egss and ham under any circumstances. However, after trying the green eggs and ham he decides he can eat them anywhere.

Try green eggs and ham. Use the following recipes to prepare green eggs and ham. (SG)

Green Eggs

8 eggs
¼ cup milk
½ teaspoon salt
Dash pepper
2 or 3 drops green food coloring
1 tablespoon butter

Break eggs one at a time in a cup. Discard egg shells. Add eggs one at a time to a large bowl. Add milk, salt, pepper, and food coloring. Beat together until mixed well. Melt butter in a 10-inch skillet over medium heat. When butter bubbles, pour the egg mixture into the skillet. Cook for 1 minute without stirring. Use a wooden spoon to stir the eggs gently. Continue cooking over medium heat, stirring often, until the eggs are cooked but still moist looking. Remove from the heat and serve right away. Makes 4 large or 8 small servings.

Green Ham

8 slices Canadian-style bacon
1 cup water
4 or 5 drops green food coloring

Mix food coloring and water. Pour over Canadian bacon placed in a shallow dish. Let stand for 5 minutes. Pour water off and dry bacon on paper towel. In a 10-inch skillet over medium-low heat, cook bacon. After the bacon begins to sizzle, cook 2 minutes on each side. Remove from heat and serve. Makes 8 servings.

Steig, William. **Brave Irene.** Farrar, Straus, and Giroux, 1986.

Irene braves a snow storm to take an evening gown made by her mother to the duchess. She is invited to stay for the ball and has a wonderful time. The duchess sends Irene home with a doctor to see about her mother, who is ill, and sends with them ginger cake with white icing, oranges, pineapple, and spiced candy of many flavors.

Ginger cake. Use a spice cake mix to make a cake and frost it with white icing. Use prepared white icing that can be purchased at the grocery store. Serve cake to the entire group. Note: Include oranges, pineapples, and spiced gum drops for additional snack foods. (SG,LG)

Tresselt, Alvin. **White Snow, Bright Snow.** Illustrated by Roger A. Duvoisin. Lothrop, Lee and Shepard, 1947. Caldecott Medal Award.

Depicts the world waiting for the season's first snowfall. Bold black and white illustrations show the first snowflakes.

Snowballs

½ cup (1 stick) butter
2 tablespoons sugar
1 tablespoon vanilla extract
1 cup all-purpose flour
1 cup chopped pecans (optional)

Cream the butter and sugar. Add flour, nuts, and vanilla. Mix well. Make into balls. Bake in a slow oven at 300 degrees for 25 minutes. Roll the cookies in powdered sugar while still warm. (SG)

Ward, Lynd. **The Biggest Bear.** Houghton-Mifflin, 1952. Caldecott Medal Award.

The story of Johnny Orchard and his dilemma when the bear cub he found in the forest and took home with him grew up to be a huge bear. The bear loved to eat, especially the maple syrup the neighbors tapped from their maple trees and the maple sugar Johnny bought at the store. The bear was saved from being shot when he was captured to be taken to a zoo in the city. Johnny always took him maple sugar when he went to visit him.

Maple syrup. Buy maple syrup at the grocery store. Serve maple syrup on waffles or pancakes. (SG,LG)

Maple sugar. Sample maple sugar. Real maple sugar can often be found at a country store or a specialty store. Although rich, maple sugar can be eaten as candy. (I,SG,LG)

Programming notes: In an area of the country where maple sugaring is practiced, take children to observe the process from tapping the sugar maple trees for sap to making the maple syrup and the maple sugar.

NOTES

[1] Patricia Barrett and Rosemary Dalton, *The Kid's Cookbook* (Concord, Calif.: Nitty Gritty Productions, 1973), 11.

[2] Terry Graham, *Let Loose on Mother Goose* (Nashville, Tenn.: Incentive Publications, 1982), 57.

[3] Patricia Barrett and Rosemary Dalton, *The Kid's Cookbook* (Concord, Calif.: Nitty Gritty Productions, 1973), 130.

[4] Imogene Forte, *Arts and Crafts: From Things Around the House* (Nashville, Tenn.: Incentive Publications, 1983), 22-23.

6
LET'S CELEBRATE
Children's Literature and Special Days of the Year

What better way to help children celebrate holidays and other special days than through the use of their literature? One finds many literature titles to accompany special days and to encourage children's celebrations. Experiencing this literature gives children information to help them better understand the holidays and to provide a broader basis for their celebrations. The ways the literary characters celebrate special days can stimulate children's imagination and creativity in their own celebrations.

School-age children love to have a party. Very simple suggestions can spark a variety of creative responses if materials and time are provided and children are encouraged to respond with their own ideas.

Programming suggestions in this chapter are intended to include the entire group in a variety of activities. The literature book, story, or poem can be presented to the entire group in a large group setting. Then most of the activities suggested are for small groups. The celebration occurs as children participate in the activities, more than one if they have time, and then come back to the large group to share or put the celebration together.

The ideas in this chapter lend themselves well to unit/theme planning as presented in the "Programming for School-Age Child Care" chapter. The public and school librarian who sees children on a regular basis but not every day needs to select activities that can be finished in one visit or session. The school-age child care teacher and classroom teacher, however, might extend the theme and celebration preparation over several days since they see the children every day. Librarians and teachers are encouraged to add their own ideas to the activities suggested here and to encourage children to share ideas for celebrating, too.

Many new ideas are presented in this chapter; in addition, reference is given to suggestions in preceding chapters that provide activities for the selected celebrations. A variety of special days and holidays are presented in this chapter. In addition, teachers and librarians are encouraged to develop themes appropriate for celebrating special days in their own location.

VALUES OF USING LITERATURE BASED ACTIVITIES FOR SPECIAL DAYS OF THE YEAR

- To provide for an extension of the sheer enjoyment of the literature.

- To help and encourage creative imagination.

- To encourage growth in social understanding and cooperation.

- To help children be aware of the materials available for their information and enjoyment to help them celebrate the special events of the year.

TECHNIQUES FOR CELEBRATING WITH CHILDREN'S LITERATURE

- Use the same techniques as in the preceding sections for "Let's Celebrate" that call for art, creative dramatics, music, and cooking.

- Find new ideas that will not duplicate home and school activities, unless children request duplications.

- Plan ahead so materials can be secured for special activities on special days when they will be in demand.

- Keep a notebook or file of titles available and related activities used.

- Refer to the preceding sections for many of the "Let's Celebrate" activities.

METHODS OF EVALUATION

- Do children seek literature titles when holidays are coming up?

- Are children becoming more aware of what is available to them and where they can find it?

- Do children seem to enjoy and want to do more and read more about the special days?

- Observe the children's use of ideas from experiences with the suggested activities as a basis for other creative ways to celebrate holidays and special events.

CHILDREN'S LITERATURE AND SPECIAL DAYS OF THE YEAR

January

NEW YEAR'S DAY—January 1
   Celebrate the first day of the new year. This is the day to make resolutions, hang a new calendar, and have a party with friends.

Anno, Mitsumasa, Raymond Briggs, Ron Brooks, Eric Carle, Gian Calvi, Zhu Chengliang, Leo Dillon, Diane Dillon, Akiko Hayashi, and Nicolai Ye. Popov. **All in a Day.** Philomel, 1986.
   Illustrations of ten internationally known artists and children's book illustrators reveal New Year's Day in the lives of children in eight different countries. Similarities and differences, with emphasis on the commonality of humankind, are presented. The distinct style of each artist is evident. Differences in time and weather in each location are depicted. Geographic information is included for parents, teachers, and older readers. Brief biographical information for each artist is given. Nine illustrations on a double-page spread make this title more appropriate for use by individuals or a small group of children at one time.
   New Year's Day around the world. Locate each illustrated location on a map or globe. Select one or more of the countries to learn more about. Learn about its customs, celebrations, dress, foods, and games for children. Specifically duplicate some of the New Year's celebrations for the country chosen. Use this book as a basis for a unit or units on other lands. (I,SG,LG)
   Illustrator study. Locate other books the illustrators of this book have done. The Dillons, for example, have illustrated several picture books of African stories and subjects. Do an author/illustrator study; find some biographic information and as many of their books as possible to read and examine. (I,SG,LG)

78 / LET'S CELEBRATE

The following list identifies titles by several of the authors/illustrators:

Anno (Italy)

Anno, Mitsumasa. *Anno's Alphabet.* Crowell, 1975.
_____ . *Anno's Counting Book.* Crowell, 1975.
_____ . *Anno's Journey.* Collins-World, 1978.
_____ . *Anno's U.S.A.* Philomel, 1983.

Raymond Briggs (England)

Briggs, Raymond. *Father Christmas.* Coward, McCann, and Geoghegan, 1973.
_____ . *Fee Fi Fo Fum.* Coward, McCann, and Geoghegan, 1964.
_____ . *Jim and the Beanstalk.* Coward, McCann, and Geoghegan, 1970.
_____ . *Ring-A-Ring O' Roses.* Coward, McCann, and Geoghegan, 1962.
_____ . *The Snowman.* Random House, 1978.

Ron Brooks (Australia)

Brooks, Ron. *Timothy and Gramps.* Bradbury Press, 1978.
Wagner, Jenny. *Aranea.* Illustrated by Ron Brooks. Bradbury Press, 1978.
_____ . *The Bunyip of Berkeley's Creek.* Illustrated by Ron Brooks. Bradbury Press, 1977.
_____ . *John Brown, Rose and the Midnight Cat.* Illustrated by Ron Brooks. Bradbury Press, 1978.

Eric Carle (U.S.A.)

Carle, Eric. *Do You Want to Be My Friend?* Crowell, 1971.
_____ . *The Grouchy Ladybug.* Crowell, 1977.
_____ . *The Mixed-up Chameleon.* rev. ed. Crowell, 1984.
_____ . *1, 2, 3 to the Zoo.* Collins-World, 1969.
_____ . *The Tiny Seed.* Crowell, 1970.
_____ . *The Very Hungry Caterpillar.* Collins-World, 1969.

Leo Dillon and Diane Dillon (Kenya)

Aardema, Verna. *Who's in Rabbit's House.* Illustrated by Leo Dillon and Diane Dillon. Dial, 1977.
Aardema, Verna. *Why Mosquitoes Buzz in People's Ears.* Illustrated by Leo Dillon and Diane Dillon, Dial, 1975. Caldecott Medal Award.

Brustlein, Janice. **Little Bear's New Year's Party.** Illustrated by Mariana Curtis Foster. Lothrop, Lee, and Shepard, 1973.
Little Bear and his friends have their own New Year's party. They had never been to a New Year's party so they plan one of their own. The party is a great success even though many more guests come than are invited.
New Year's party. Plan a party for the first week in January, when everyone is back from the holidays. Decorate the room with a banner, wear hats, at appropriate times use noisemakers, and serve punch and cookies. (LG)
Banner. Make a New Year's banner. Use a large piece of paper 6 or 8 feet long. Make large block letters that say HAPPY NEW YEAR. Allow children to use their own ideas to decorate banner with stars, drawings, designs, and colorful paper. (SG)

Hats. Have available construction paper (12 by 18 inches), tissue paper, markers, stapler, and glue. Make simple or elaborate hats. A simple hat is made by cutting a band of paper 5 by 18 inches. Fit band to head. Remove and staple the two ends together at the correct size. Decorate the band as desired. Add tissue paper for decoration or inside the diameter for the crown. Variation: Make a cone hat. Use a 12-by-18-inch piece of construction paper. Cut base for cone as shown.

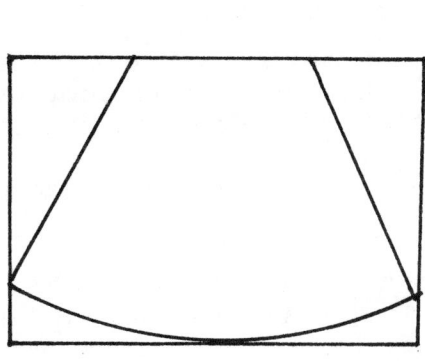

Decorate base of cone. Form cone to fit head. Glue together. Attach elastic or string on each side of hat above ears to hold hat on head. Add a feather or streamers at point for decoration. (I,SG)

Noisemakers. Have available sturdy paper plates, small pebbles or beans, and crepe paper. Make shaker-like noisemakers by placing small pebbles or beans inside two paper plates and stapling them together. Add streamers of crepe paper for decoration. (I,SG)

Other noisemakers.

- Pie tins with pop bottle caps attached for tambourines.

- Band-Aid boxes with small pebbles or beans for shakers. Cover with colorful adhesive paper.

- Toilet tissue rolls closed at both ends by stapling one end together adding pebbles, rice, or beans and then stapling the other end. Add streamers for decoration. Variation: Use small concentrated frozen juice cans cut open at both ends. Wrap with tissue paper. Tie one end with yarn. Add small pebbles and treats (candy or trinkets) then tie the other end. Hand out as favors at the party.

Additional ideas: Make streamers from crepe paper. Make confetti by cutting paper or punching holes from paper.

Resolutions bulletin board. Discuss resolutions and the value of making resolutions at the beginning of a new year. Encourage children to make their own resolutions. On a half sheet of paper for each child, record his resolution, or have the children draw pictures of their resolutions. Arrange on bulletin board around the title "New Year's Resolutions." Note: Resolutions can be signed or unsigned. Children may choose not to post resolutions that are too personal. (SG,LG)

80 / LET'S CELEBRATE

Calendars. Make a large January calendar for room and/or individual calendars. Help children block off calendar and number days. Write or draw in special dates, activities, and birthdays. For the classroom calendar, use a piece of heavy poster paper. Use 8-by-11½-inch paper for individual calendars. Note: Children may wish to make calendars each month. This is a good way for children to help plan and know what is planned. Calendars also inform parents of planned events. (I,SG)

Additional New Year's title:

Modell, Frank. *Goodbye Old Year, Hello New Year.* Greenwillow, 1984.

Programming notes: The activities presented here may take several days to complete. Encourage children to choose and work in small groups during the choice of activity time to make preparations for the New Year's party. They may have time to participate in more than one activity. Set a certain day and time for the party.

One or a combination of activities may be chosen for a one-session New Year's celebration.

THREE KINGS' DAY — January 6

Three Kings' Day (Epiphany) celebrates the day the wise men brought gifts to Jesus. For years people have celebrated this day by baking a special "king's cake." A cake is baked with a small trinket crown or bean in it. The one who finds the trinket or bean becomes the "king" for the day.

De Paola, Tomie. **The Story of the Three Wise Kings.** Putnam's Sons, 1983.

The story of the wise men who went to Bethlehem to see Jesus is retold. The kings brought gifts of gold, frankincense, and myrrh. The story is simply told and beautifully illustrated.

King's cake. Make cupcakes. Use a cake mix. Follow the directions for cupcakes. In the bottom of one cupcake liner before baking, place a dried bean. Bake and ice cupcakes. Serve for snack. Remember, the child who has the bean in his/her cupcake becomes "king" for the day. Have a small group of two or three children make the cupcakes to share with the entire group. (I,SG)

Crowns. Have construction paper (12 by 18 inches), markers, and foil paper available. Cut a band 5 or 6 inches by 18 inches. Allow children to decorate their own crowns. Make the most elaborate crown for the king for the day. Adjust crown to appropriate head size and staple ends together. (I,SG)

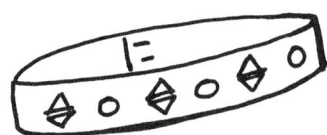

If I were king .... Lead a discussion of what each child would do if he were a king. Write the responses on poster board or chart paper to be posted in the room. (SG,LG)

Additional wise men title:

Menotti, Gian Carlo. *Amahl and the Night Visitors.* Illustrated by Michéle Lemieux. Morrow, 1986.

Dramatize the story. See suggestions for this title in the "Let's Pretend" chapter. (SG)

JAPANESE NEW YEAR

The Japanese New Year is celebrated the first week in January. Homes are decorated and the time becomes a festive occasion. This is a special time for Japanese children. They play many games and especially enjoy kite flying.

Yashima, Taro. **Crow Boy.** Viking, 1955. Caldecott Honor Book.

A shy Japanese mountain boy is a lonely outcast at school. A sensitive teacher recognizes his potential and helps him gain self-confidence. He is called Crow Boy because of his special talent to imitate crows.

Japanese Kite. Children celebrate the Japanese New Year by flying kites. Make a Japanese fish kite. Look for a children's kite-making book in your public library or use the simple directions found in *Happy Holidays* by White and Kusion-Rowe.[1] (I,SG)

Sock kites. Have available a piece of tagboard, very lightweight pellon or fabric, string, and a stick. Make a band by stapling together a 2-by-20-inch strip of tagboard. Fold a 21-by-12-inch piece of material, lengthwise. Overlapping ½ inch, glue 12-inch edge of fabric together. When dry, turn sock, and attach one open end to tagboard band with glue. Add streamers of material to the other end of sock. Secure one end of a 24-by-36-inch string to the top of the "sock" and the other to the stick. Sock can be hung vertically to blow in the wind or child can hold the stick and run with the sock kite. Decorate the kite. Different colors of material can be used or markers draw well on pellon. (I,SG)

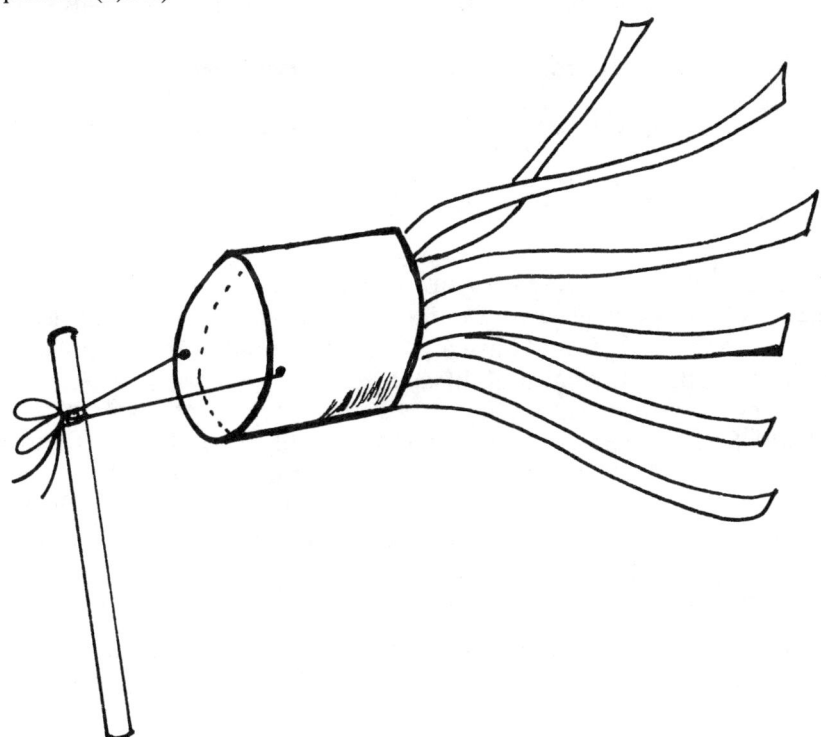

Japanese origami. Use origami as suggested in "Let's Create" as an extension of *Crow Boy*. Use this Japanese folding technique to make paper birds (crows). (SG)

Charades. Have children select an animal they would like to be. Allow them to take turns using motions and sounds to help their peers and teacher guess what they are. (SG,LG)

82 / LET'S CELEBRATE

Programming notes: In connection with the Japanese New Year celebration or in response to a travel or other lands unit, use a Japanese theme. Several days can be spent on different aspects of this country. In addition to the activities above consider the following:

- Bulletin board display of pictures from Japan depicting Japanese life.

- Display of Japanese costumes, toys, figurines, fans, and writing samples.

- Play Japanese children's games found in books suggesting games of children from other lands.

- Have a native of Japan visit to share culture.

- Make and decorate own Japanese fans.

- Practice writing Japanese written characters.

- Visit a Japanese garden. Learn about the Bonsai tree and shrubs.

Additional titles on Japan:

Bang, Molly. *The Paper Crane.* Greenwillow, 1985.

Heller, George. *Hiroshi's Wonderful Kite.* Illustrated by Kyuzo Tsugami. Silver Burdett, 1968.

McDermott, Gerald. *The Stonecutter: A Japanese Folk Tale.* Viking, 1975.

Mosel, Arlene. *The Funny Little Woman.* Illustrated by Blair Lent. Dutton, 1972.

Yashima, Taro. *Umbrella.* Viking, 1958.

CHINESE NEW YEAR

The Chinese New Year is celebrated for fifteen days in January or February, according to where it falls on the calendar. This is a festive celebration for the Chinese people. They clean and decorate their houses, hang lanterns in the streets, and have a parade. Celebrating special holidays of other cultures helps children begin to understand cultural differences.

Mosel, Arlene. **Tikki Tikki Tembo.** Illustrated by Blair Lent. Holt, Rinehart and Winston, 1968.

A Chinese folk tale that relates why the Chinese give all their children short names. Because of his long name, Tikki Tikki Tembo almost drowned when he fell in the well and it took his brother so long to say his name. The illustrations depict Chinese life and dress.

Chinese New Year's parade. Make a Chinese dragon, lanterns, flags, and banners for the parade. See directions in the "Let's Create" chapter under *Tikki Tikki Tembo.* (LG)

Programming notes: Read and view stories about dragons to help children visualize what dragons might look like. Children may choose to make a large dragon for the parade or an individual one using egg cartons, green tempera paint, fabric scraps, and other art materials.

Suggested dragon titles:

Grahame, Kenneth. *The Reluctant Dragon.* Illustrated by Ernest H. Shepard. Holiday House, 1938.

Hodges, Margaret. *Saint George and the Dragon.* Illustrated by Trina Schart Hyman. Little, Brown, & Co., 1984. Caldecott Medal Award.

Mahy, Margaret. *The Dragon of an Ordinary Family.* Illustrated by Helen Oxenbury. Watts, 1969.

Williams, Jay. *Everyone Knows What a Dragon Looks Like.* Illustrated by Mercer Mayer. Four Winds, 1976.

Chinese music. Select Chinese music for background music for the parade. Have drums, cymbals, and wrist or ankle bells to provide music for the parade. (SG,LG)

Chinese food. Sample Chinese food such as egg rolls, egg drop soup, Chinese noodles, and fortune cookies. Use chopsticks for eating food. (LG)

Programming notes: Like the theme on Japan, develop a theme on China. Use some of the following additional ideas:

- Visit a Chinese restaurant.

- Invite a person of Chinese origin to visit the program. Ask the visitor to share information about the culture, celebrations, and customs.

- Have a display of Chinese art, writing, costumes, and figurines.

- Play Chinese checkers.

CHARLES PERRAULT DAY—January 12

January 12 is the birthday of Charles Perrault, considered the "father of fairy tales." Born in 1628 in France, he is believed to be the first person to record many of the fairy tales in a collection called *Tales of Mother Goose.* Many adaptations of his fairy tales exist today. The day can be celebrated by reading a variety of these fairy tales. Find titles that are available in your library.

Charles Perrault fairy tales:

Perrault, Charles. *Cinderella.* Illustrated by Marcia Brown. Scribner, 1954.

_____ . *The Glass Slipper.* Translated by John Bierhorst. Illustrated by Mitchell Miller. Four Winds, 1981.

_____ . *Puss in Boots.* Illustrated by Marcia Brown. Scribner, 1952.

_____ . *Puss in Boots.* Illustrated by Hans Fischer. Harcourt, Brace, Jovanovich, 1959.

_____ . *The Sleeping Beauty.* Translated and illustrated by David Walker. Crowell, 1977.

Activities to extend children's experiences with fairy tales are numerous. Some suggestions are presented here. Teachers are encouraged to add to this list. The best management seems to be to select several activities. Allow children to participate in one of the activities with small groups then share experiences with the whole group. The small and large group process should take about an hour.

Present fairy tales. Have Perrault fairy tales available. Read three or four fairy tales or have children who can read select and read for themselves. Discuss the fairy tales—characters, action, plot. Allow children to select the ones liked best. (LG)

Favorite fairy tale. Have children draw or paint a scene from their favorite fairy tales. Display these pictures on the classroom bulletin board. (I,SG)

Puppets. Make paper bag, paper plate, or stick puppets of favorite fairy tale characters. Put on a puppet show acting out favorite scenes or the entire story. (SG)

Play. Select favorite fairy tale. Use dress-up clothes and costumes. Make or find simple props for selected story. Practice, then act out for the group favorite scenes or the whole fairy tale. Variations: Act out, charade style, a selected character for children to guess who it is. Or pose a scene(s) of a favorite fairy tale for children to guess the scene and characters. (SG)

84 / LET'S CELEBRATE

Programming notes: Once a month have an author/illustrator day. The day might be designated by an author/illustrator's actual birthday. Share selected books, stories, or poems in appropriate ways. Consult this guide for ways to extend children's experiences with their literature. Have books available in the book center or on display for children to check out.

February

GROUNDHOG DAY – February 2
   On February 2 around 7:00 AM, if the groundhog sees his shadow and runs back into his hole, there will be six more weeks of winter weather before spring. If he does not see his shadow, spring is on the way.

Cohen, Carol. **Wake Up, Groundhog!** Crown, 1975.
   The adventures of Groundhog on Groundhog Day.
   Field trip. Go outside in the early morning. Do you see your shadow? This can be an assignment for children. (I,SG,LG)
   Shadows. Provide a bright light (gooseneck or filmstrip projector lamp) shown against a white background. Put hands in front of the light. Using hands, make shadows of different animals and objects. (I,SG)
   Shadow game. Play a shadow chase game. Select children to chase and be chased. When the shadows of children being chased are stepped on, they are out of the game. Continue until all are caught. (SG,LG)

   Additional shadow activities:

See the "Let's Create" chapter for art activities suggested for Blaise Cendrars's *Shadow*.

ABRAHAM LINCOLN'S BIRTHDAY – February 12
   Abraham Lincoln was born in Kentucky on February 12, 1809. Because his family was poor, he lived in a log cabin. He later became president of the United States.

D'Aulaire, Ingri, and Edgar P. D'Aulaire. **Abraham Lincoln.** Doubleday, 1939. Caldecott Medal Award.
   The life of Abraham Lincoln from boyhood through adult achievements. Illustrations provide a realistic depiction of Lincoln's life.
   Log cabins. See directions in "Let's Create" chapter under Donald Hall's *Ox-Cart Man*.
   Lincoln penny rubbings. Have available pennies, newsprint, and pencil or copper colored crayon. Secure a penny or pennies to a table or cardboard by placing a loop of tape under each penny. Place the newsprint over the penny. Rub with a pencil or copper colored crayon. Make as many rubbings in as many designs as desired. (I,SG)

   Alternate title:

Cavanah, Frances. *Abe Lincoln Gets His Chance.* Illustrated by Don Sibley. Scholastic, Inc., n.d.
   A warm, fictionalized story of Lincoln's life before becoming president. Provides a good read aloud selection for young school-age children.

VALENTINE'S DAY – February 14
   For centuries Valentine's Day has been celebrated by exchanging pretty cards and special messages.

Cohen, Miriam. **Bee My Valentine!** Illustrated by Lillian Hoban. Greenwillow, 1978.

Special story of a first grade class valentine celebration. Some of the children get many Valentines and are happy, but some get few and are displeased. George is so unhappy that he cries in the coat room until some of his classmates make him feel better.

Valentines. Have white and red construction paper, wallpaper samples, or wrapping paper; and pencil or felt tipped marker available. Cut hearts from red construction paper, wallpaper samples, or wrapping paper. Glue on folded piece of paper. Write valentine message on the inside. (I,SG)

Valentine collage. Have available construction paper or wallpaper samples, and collage materials such as lace, beads, and doilies. Cut a large valentine from construction paper or wallpaper samples. Glue lace, beads, doilies, other collage items, and other valentines of different shapes and colors to the large valentine. Everyone's will be different. (I,SG)

Valentine collection box. Use a large box. Cut a slot in the top to drop in valentines. Cover the box with white paper. Have children decorate the box. Add crepe paper, glue on valentines, draw valentines, and write messages. This project should be done several days before Valentine's Day so children will have a place to deposit their valentines as they make them. (LG)

Valentine party. Serve red punch and valentine cookies. Use butter cookie recipe in "Let's Cook" chapter suggested under Eve Bunting's *St. Patrick's Day in the Morning.* Of course, use heart shaped cookie cutters and sprinkle with red sugar. Have two or three children make the cookies or provide an opportunity for each child to roll out dough and cut out his own cookie(s). Assign one or two children to keep up with the baking time. (SG,LG)

Special valentines. Select a senior citizen, or community or school helper. Make Valentines for this person. Deliver valentines (include a package of cookies) to this special person. (SG,LG)

De Paola, Tomie. **Things to Make and Do for Valentine's Day.** Watts, 1967. (Scholastic, 1967).

A Valentine's Day activity book for children. Includes ideas for celebrating Valentine's Day by making cards and decorations, party refreshments, presents, and playing games. Illustrations and step-by-step directions are easy for children to follow. Ideas in this book are all one would need for a super Valentine's celebration.

Things to make. Use the ideas in this book to make the following:

Valentine cards—A number of illustrations are included to spark ideas for making a variety of cards. (I,SG)

Printed Valentines—Detailed directions are given for printed Valentines using styrofoam trays. (I,SG)

Mailbag—Directions are given for each child to make his or her own Valentine mailbag. (I,SG)

Table decorations. Use the decoration ideas for a Valentine tree for table decorations. (SG)

Valentine messages and jokes. Use the Valentine messages and jokes or make up original ones for Valentine cards. (I,SG)

Valentine party. Have a party on Valentine's Day. Use the recipes and directions given for sandwiches and a chocolate snowball dessert. (SG,LG)

Valentine party games. Use the two games suggested, a relay race and a card trick. (SG)

Valentine presents. Have children make a Valentine necklace for themselves or for chosen friends. Use the Baker's Clay recipe in the book. (I,SG)

Additional actitivies:

Valentine bulletin board. Provide red and white construction paper and felt tipped markers. Use the caption "Love is .... " Have children write one word on each cut out valentine to place on the bulletin board. (SG,LG)

86 / LET'S CELEBRATE

    Concentration game. Make pairs of valentines, as many different pairs as children can think of. Make all the backs the same. To play the game, spread the valentines out face down. Take turns trying to match pairs. The player with the most matching pairs is the winner at the end of the game. (I,SG)

    Additional Valentine titles:

Brown, Marc. *Arthur's Valentine.* Little, Brown, & Co., 1980.

Nixon, Joan Lowery. *The Valentine Mystery.* Illustrated by Jim Cummins. Whitman, 1979.

Wahl, Jan. *Pleasant Fieldmouse's Valentine Trick.* Illustrated by Erik Belgvad. Dutton, 1977.

GEORGE WASHINGTON'S BIRTHDAY — February 22
    George Washington was born on February 22, 1732. He was a plantation owner and the first president of the United States. He is a very important person for children to know about and whose birthday they can celebrate.

D'Aulaire, Ingri, and Edgar P. D'Aulaire. **George Washington.** Doubleday, 1936.
    The story of George Washington from a boy to the first president of the United States. Illustrations appropriately depict Washington's life.

Flag of the Thirteen Colonies. Secure red, white, and blue construction paper. Consult an encyclopedia or other resource to identify the arrangement of the stars and stripes of the flag of the thirteen colonies. Make the flag with thirteen stripes (seven red, six white) and thirteen stars arranged in a circle on the blue background. (I,SG)

Three-cornered hat. Have on hand black construction paper, pencil, scissors, and staples. Cut three of the sides of the hat from black construction paper. Staple ends together to form the three-cornered hat.[2] (I,SG)

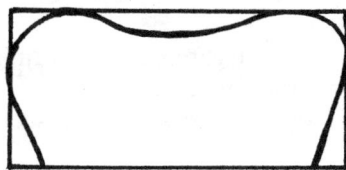

Cherry tart. See Ingri D'Aulaire and Edgar D'Aulaire's *George Washington* in the chapter "Let's Cook."

March

ST. PATRICK'S DAY—March 17

This day is set aside in honor of the patron saint of Ireland, St. Patrick. He is honored for the many good things legends say he did for the people of Ireland. He is believed to have driven the snakes from Ireland and taught the people Christianity and to read and write.

Cantwell, Mary. **St. Patrick's Day.** Illustrated by Ursula Arndt. Crowell, 1967.

Factual information about St. Patrick's Day is incorporated into the story about St. Patrick.

Wear green. Dress in green and cut out a green shamrock to pin on each person who doesn't so no one will be pinched by a leprechaun. (I)

Shamrock cookies. See "Let's Cook" under Eve Bunting's *St. Patrick's Day in the Morning* for cookie recipe.

Programming notes: Add some of the following suggestions to the ones above for a fun St. Patrick's Day celebration.

- Play I spy, identifying things that are green in the room.

- Have a parade or go to a parade if your community has one and the time is right.

- Look up recipes for Irish potatoes and Irish soda bread. Prepare and serve for snack.

- Take a walk around the school. Have children make a list of all the things they find that are green. Who has the longest list?

Additional St. Patrick titles:

Bunting, Eve. *St. Patrick's Day in the Morning.* Illustrated by Jan Brett. Houghton-Mifflin, 1980.

Kessel, Joyce K. *St. Patrick's Day.* Illustrated by Cathy Gilchrist. Carolrhoda, 1982.

88 / LET'S CELEBRATE

FIRST DAY OF SPRING—March 20 or 21
    March 20 or 21, when the sun crosses the equator from south to north, is the first day of spring.

Ets, Marie Hall. **Gilberto and the Wind.** Viking, 1963.
    The story of a Mexican boy, Gilberto, and his experiences with a kite and the wind. The wind becomes Gilberto's playmate.
    Kite. Use directions in "Let's Create" chapter under this title for a simple kite or in this chapter celebrating the Japanese New Year for a more elaborate kite. Also, consult books in your library that give kite making directions. Provide time to try kites out on a windy day. (I,SG)

Zion, Gene. **Really Spring.** Illustrated by Margaret B. Graham. Harper & Row, 1956.
    The children paint their own spring when they become tired of waiting for spring to come. The pen-and-ink illustrations add pastel colors to life's scenes and the children paint their own spring.
    Paint a springtime picture. See the "Let's Create" chapter for directions for Gene Zion's *Really Spring.*
    Observe signs of spring. Take a walk in the community or local park. Make a note of all the changes from winter to spring. Listen to the sounds of spring. Are the smells of spring different? Note: Teacher should make a previous visit to the area to know what to expect. (SG,LG)
    Plant a garden. If space is available, children may wish to plant a vegetable or flower garden. This will give them opportunity to use real tools and do real work. Note: If space is not available, plant a tub or box garden. (SG,LG)

    Programming notes: Include some of these additional ideas in program planning.

- Visit a seed store.

- Visit a farm to see new life in the spring and springtime activities.

- Visit a greenhouse.

April

APRIL FOOL'S DAY—April 1
    The first day of April is observed as April Fool's Day. Where or when the day originated is unknown, but it is celebrated in many countries. On this day, friends may play practical jokes on each other or try to make what they say convincing. The one who is tricked is the April fool.

McKie, Roy. **The Riddle Book.** Random House, 1978.
    Simple riddles to delight children in first and second grades, such as this:

Question: "What is worse than a centipede with sore feet?"
Answer: "A giraffe with a sore throat."
                              or
Question: "How does a monster count to thirteen?"
Answer: "On its fingers"

Illustrations are included for each riddle.
    Original riddles. Have a contest. See who can make the best riddle to share with the class. Have children write and illustrate their riddles. Make a book or bulletin board using the original riddles. Note: First and second grade children love riddles. (I,SG,LG)

Scheer, Julian. **Upside Down Day.** Illustrated by Kelly Oechsli. Holiday House, 1968.

On an upside-down day things do not happen as they usually do. For example, "Bees won't sting" and "Bells won't ring." The text and illustrations include many examples of reverses of what usually happens.

Have an upside-down, backwards, or wrong-side-out day. To celebrate April Fool's Day, dress with clothes on backwards or wrong-side-out. Do other things in reverse or opposite of the way they are usually done. (SG,LG)

Opposites or reverses. Think of opposites or reverses to add to the story line and illustrations included in this title. (I,SG,LG)

Upside-down cake. For April Fool's Day, make and serve an upside-down cake. See directions in the "Let's Cook" chapter for *Upside Down Day.* (SG,LG)

Thayer, Marjorie. **The April Foolers.** Illustrated by Don Freeman. Children's Press, 1978.

An entertaining play that teaches an important lesson in the difference between a cruel joke and a funny one. Written in play form appropriate for children in second grade or older.

Play reading. After reading the play to the group, provide several copies of the book. Assign parts to members of the group. Read the play as written. Note: After reading the play several times, children might choose to act it out. (SG)

EASTER

Easter is the first Sunday after the first full moon occurring on or after March 21. The religious emphasis celebrates the death and resurrection of Jesus Christ. This time of the year is also a celebration of spring and new life.

Adams, Adrienne. **The Easter Egg Artists.** Scribner, 1976.

A rabbit family paints designs on Easter eggs. Orson, the son, prefers big projects to Easter eggs. He paints designs on a house, bridge, and other things including a new product for the family business, decorated ostrich eggs.

Think big. Use poster board and markers or paints. Cut out a big egg from poster board. Decide on individual design and decorate the egg. Everyone's egg should be different. Display finished products in the room. (I,SG)

Dye eggs. Boil eggs. Use commercial egg dye or food coloring. Follow directions on package for dye preparation and egg dying. (SG)

Decorate eggs. Use decals, small bits of paper and glue, or markers to decorate eggs. Caution: If eggs are to be eaten, do not use decorating materials like oil paint and permanent markers. (SG)

Egg hunt. Hide and hunt eggs. Use a plastic egg with a treat inside as a prize that may be kept by the child who finds it. Children may take turns hiding eggs. Even the hardest hiding places are not difficult for school-age children. (LG)

Langstaff, John. **Hot Cross Buns and Other Old Street Cries.** Illustrated by Nancy Winslow Parker. Atheneum, 1978.

Includes "Hot Cross Buns" and other English street chants. Hot cross buns are an English tradition at Easter time. School-age children love chants and rhymes.

Hot cross buns. See "Let's Cook" chapter under John Langstaff's *Hot Cross Buns and Other Old Street Cries* for directions.

Lionni, Leo. **Let's Make Rabbits.** Pantheon Books, 1982.

A delightful story of two rabbits—a pencil rabbit and a scissors rabbit—and their friendship.

Rabbits. Make scissors rabbits and pencil rabbits. Directions are found in "Let's Create" chapter under Lionni.

90 / LET'S CELEBRATE

Additional Easter and rabbit titles:

Brown, Margaret Wise. *The Golden Egg Book.* Illustrated by Leonard Weisgard. Simon and Schuster, 1947.

Brown, Margaret Wise. *The Runaway Bunny.* Illustrated by Clement Hurd. Harper & Row, 1942.

Stevenson, James. *The Great Big Especially Beautiful Easter Egg.* Greenwillow, 1983.

Zolotow, Charlotte. *The Bunny Who Found Easter.* Illustrated by Betty F. Peterson. Parnassus, 1959.

ARBOR DAY – April 22

The original Arbor Day is April 22. This day may be celebrated on different dates in different states. It is a day that trees are planted to replace trees in the forest or to beautify the community.

Tresselt, Alvin. **Johnny Maple-Leaf.** Illustrated by Roger A. Duvoisin. Lothrop, Lee and Shepard, 1948.

The story of Johnny Maple-Leaf follows him through the seasons. A good story line as well as factual information about the change of the maple leaf from season to season.

Collect leaves. Use leaves for art activities such as leaf rubbings, leaf melt, or leaf mobile. See directions for these activities in the "Let's Create" chapter under this title.

Leaf Collection. When leaves are mature in the spring, collect and press a variety of leaves. Mount different pressed leaves on plain paper. Identify each leaf. Write the name of the leaf by the leaf. Make a cover of construction paper. Staple together on the side or punch two holes and connect with yarn. Note: Each child may choose this activity or only a few may be involved. The collection will take several days to complete. (I,SG,LG)

Udry, Janice. **A Tree Is Nice.** Illustrated by Marc Simont. Harper & Row, 1956. Caldecott Award Book.

Brilliant tempera illustrations of a tree through the seasons of the year. The story line depicts many useful functions of trees.

Tree walk. Walk around the area of the school. Identify the different trees growing in the area. This is a good experience for all the children, especially with a "tree expert" – someone who knows about trees' identities and uses. (SG,LG)

Create trees. Use torn paper collage and sponge painting art activities suggested in "Let's Create" for this title.

Plant a tree. If space and opportunity are available, plant a tree near school. Water it and watch it grow. Note: Indoor trees may be grown by planting fresh citrus seeds in soil (orange, grapefruit, lemon). Be sure to place in a sunny spot. Water and be patient. The seed takes about six weeks. (SG,LG)

Programming notes: Plan an Arbor Day celebration. Select activities suggested above as well as some of the ones included below. Allow children to choose activities when possible and involve all in group activities.

- Visit a tree and shrub nursery.

- Invite forestry service representatives to visit group. Meet in a park or wooded area so representative can share firsthand information.

- Visit a construction site to observe an important use of wood.

- Use wood scraps, nails, glue, and hammers for supervised carpentry activity.

May

MOTHER'S DAY

Mother's Day is observed the second Sunday in May.

Kroll, Steven. **Happy Mother's Day.** Illustrated by Marilyn Hafner. Holiday House, 1985.

An excellent Mother's Day book for school-age children. On Mother's Day, Mom finds surprise presents throughout the house. Various clues leads her to a clean room, a necklace made at school, and a great dinner on the table, and many other gifts that are special to mother and do not cost money. The children and their father planned these surprises.

Surprises for mother. Encourage children to plan surprises and clues for their mother on Mother's Day. A group discussion after reading this story might help children select some ideas. Help each child make a list of things he or she might do. Give children time and help to write their clues at school. (I,LG)

Williams, Vera B. **A Chair for My Mother.** Morrow, 1982. Caldecott Honor Book.

After a fire destroys their furniture, a young girl helps her waitress mother and grandmother save money for a new chair. The appealing illustrations depict the love the girl, her mother, and her grandmother have for each other.

Mother's Day card. Provide a variety of art materials and plain white paper. Make Mother's Day cards using a choice of techniques—drawing with crayons or magic markers, collage, rubbings, stenciling, or painting. Fold the plain paper and decorate the outside. On the inside write a special Mother's Day message. (I,SG,LG)

Collage vase. Have available tissue paper, diluted glue, and small, empty bottles or cans. Save empty salad dressing bottles, mayonnaise jars, or other small containers. Cut or tear tissue paper in small pieces. Apply tissue pieces to outside of container with diluted glue. Overlap paper making sure that all areas are covered. Brush a coat of diluted glue over the entire vase after all the tissue paper is applied. Note: The same process can be used by using masking tape torn and applied, small pieces at a time. Antique by brushing with diluted brown tempera or brown liquid shoe polish. (I,SG)

Coupon book. Have available wallpaper samples, colored construction paper, and plain white paper. Make a small 2-by-6-inch booklet with a colorful cover using wallpaper or construction paper. The inside pages should be of plain paper. Staple the book together at one end. On each page of the booklet the child can make redeemable coupons for mother to use. Ideas for coupons include make the bed, do the dishes, get the paper, good for one hug, and clean up my room. (I,SG)

Additional titles about mothers:

Brown, Margaret Wise. *The Runaway Bunny.* Illustrated by Clement Hurd. Harper & Row, 1942.

Moncure, Jane B. *Our Mother's Day Book.* Illustrated by Mina G. McLean. Child's World, 1977.

Polushkin, Maria. *Mother, Mother, I Want Another.* Illustrated by Diane Dawson. Crown Publishers, 1978.

Viorst, Judith. *My Mama Says ...* Atheneum, 1973.

Wells, Rosemary. *Hazel's Amazing Mother.* Dial, 1985.

Programming notes: Have children suggest other things they would like to make for their mothers. Provide materials for these suggestions if possible. Give children a choice of what they would like to make. Caution: Be sensitive to children who do not live with their mothers. You may help children select a grandmother or another person to make a gift or card for.

92 / LET'S CELEBRATE

Additional activities for Mother's Day theme:

- Visit a mother's workplace.

- Have a mother visit the group to share a special talent, collection, hobby, or interest.

- Invite a mother and her baby to visit. Have her talk about the things she likes about being a mother.

June

FLAG DAY — June 14
   The Continental Congress made the Stars and Stripes the official flag of the United States, June 14, 1777. Betsy Ross is believed to have created the first flag. The first flag had thirteen stars and thirteen stripes to represent the original thirteen colonies. How does our flag today differ from the 1777 flag? Flag Day is celebrated each June 14.

Spier, Peter. **Star-Spangled Banner.** Doubleday, 1973.
   Words of the song illustrated in a single song picture book. These words are the words of our national anthem.
   Observe United States flag. Have children look at the flag of the United States. Identify its colors and other characteristics. How many stars and stripes does it have? What do they stand for? How does it differ from the original flag? (SG,LG)
   State flag. Find out about your own state flag. Have a state flag for display. (I,SG,LG)
   Sing "The Star-Spangled Banner." Practice singing "The Star-Spangled Banner" or listen to a recording of this song. Because of the high notes this is sometimes a difficult song for children to sing. (LG)
   Make a flag. Use directions in "Let's Create" under this title to make a flag.
   Flag parade. After flags are completed, have a parade as suggested for Peter Spier's *Star-Spangled Banner* in the chapter "Let's Make Music."

FATHER'S DAY
   Father's Day is celebrated on the third Sunday in June.

Steptoe, John. **Daddy Is a Monster ... Sometimes.** Lippincott, 1980.
   The children know that Daddy loves them even though he seems like a monster when they are messy, noisy, or bothersome at bedtime. A father's love for his children is depicted in a loving, humorous story.
   Father's Day card. Provide construction paper and markers. Fold a piece of construction paper in half, crosswise. Turn the paper with the fold on the left-hand side. Draw a tie on the front of the paper. Decorate the tie on the front of the card, open and write a message on the inside. (I,SG)
   Interview father. Tape an interview with father asking him what he liked to do as a boy, what he likes about work, or what are his favorite foods. Have children who wish to, share interviews with the group. (I)
   Special visitor. Invite a father to visit the class to share information about the job he does or a special hobby or interest he has. (LG)
   Special visit. Arrange to visit a child's father at his work. For example: The fire department, police station, doctor's office. Ask him to share with the group some special aspects of his job. Or visit a father's workshop. (LG)

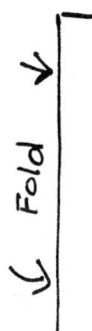 

Additional titles about fathers:

Ash, Frank. *Just Like Daddy*. Prentice-Hall, 1981.

Marzollo, Jean. *Amy Goes Fishing*. Illustrated by Ann Schweninger. Dial, 1980.

Stecher, Miriam. *Daddy and Ben Together*. Illustrated by Alice Kandell. Lothrop, Lee and Shepard, 1981.

Udry, Janice. *What Mary Jo Shared*. Illustrated by Eleanor Mill. Whitman, 1966.

July

INDEPENDENCE DAY — July 4
   Independence Day is a very special day for school-age children to celebrate. Although July 4 is a holiday and most children will be with their families, a celebration before the actual holiday is appropriate. The celebration will take some preplanning and preparation. Be sure to involve the children.

Hopkins, Lee Bennett, comp. **Beat the Drum: Independence Day Has Come.** Illustrated by Tomie De Paola. Harcourt, Brace, Jovanovich, 1977.
   A collection of poems from Carl Sandburg to Shel Silverstein on various patriotic aspects of the Fourth of July.

Keller, Holly. **Henry's Fourth of July.** Greenwillow, 1985.
   The Fourth of July is celebrated in an old-fashioned way including a parade, picnic, sack races, swimming in the pond, and fireworks. The day is too much for young Henry. He falls asleep on the way home. This story is a good reminder of the many ways the day can be celebrated.
   Flags. Make flags as suggested in the "Let's Create" chapter for Peter Spier's *Star-Spangled Banner.*
   Fireworks paintings. Use straws and diluted orange, yellow, and red paints. Drop paint on paper and blow with straws to spread the paint. Repeat with several colors. The straw painting will resemble bursts of fireworks. (I,SG)
   Picnic. Have a picnic. Allow children to help plan the menu, make a grocery list, and prepare the food. (LG)
   Relay games. Have a sack race, three-legged race, egg race, and other relay games. (LG)

94 / LET'S CELEBRATE

Additional activities for the July 4 theme:

- Spend part of a day at the park, using some of the ideas suggested above. Go swimming in the afternoon.

- Visit a local government office, like the mayor's office. Find out what the mayor does.

August

BIRTHDAYS

Birthdays can be celebrated any time of the year. August is a good time to celebrate all of the summer birthdays.

Carle, Eric. **The Secret Birthday Message.** Crowell, 1972.
    An unusual book using a code to express a birthday message. Basic shapes are used as a code to correspond to letters in the message.
    Secret code. Develop a secret code. Be sure to work out the code with the letter each symbol stands for before writing the secret message. Save the code key. Write birthday and other messages in secret code. Note: Second and third graders will enjoy this activity. They may even use the code for their club. (I,SG)

Hoban, Russell. **A Birthday for Frances.** Illustrated by Lillian Hoban. Harper & Row, 1968.
    Frances has a difficult time accepting the fact that the family is celebrating her sister Gloria's birthday and that she must wait her turn. But she does in the end.
    Party decorations. Plan a birthday party. Make decorations for the party such as a happy birthday sign, streamers, and posters. Use a theme chosen by the children such as balloons, kites, or cartoon characters. Materials needed depend on the decorations made and the theme used. (I,SG,LG)
    Place cards. Secure 4-by-6-inch index cards, felt tipped markers, and stickers. Make individual place cards for each person coming to the party. Decorate with drawings or stickers. Print a name of party guest on each card. (I,SG)

Keats, Ezra Jack. **A Letter to Amy.** Harper & Row, 1968.
    Peter writes a letter to Amy to invite her to his birthday party. He is anxious about inviting a girl but does so anyway. The illustrations show the invitation in Peter's second grade handwriting.
    Invitations. Have a birthday party. Make invitations. Decide what the invitations will say and write letter invitations for each child invited. Decorate the invitations with drawings, stickers, or as you wish. (I,SG)
    Birthday party. Make refreshments for the party. Use the birthday cookie recipe for Eric Carle's *A Secret Birthday Message* or birthday cake or ice cream cone idea for Russell Hoban's *A Birthday for Frances* in the "Let's Cook" chapter. Have some punch to drink, too. (SG,LG)

    Additional birthday titles:

Asch, Frank. *Happy Birthday Moon!* Prentice-Hall, 1982.

Elliott, Dan. *Oscar's Rotten Birthday.* Random House, 1981.

Flack, Marjorie. *Ask Mr. Bear.* Macmillan, 1932.

Hutchins, Pat. *Happy Birthday, Sam.* Greenwillow, 1978.

Programming notes: Plan a birthday party each month to celebrate birthdays for the month. Use a different birthday title each month. Plan a different theme and different ways to celebrate each month.

September

LABOR DAY

Labor Day is the first Monday in September. This is a holiday for all workers. It is a special day to say thank you to the people in the community labor force. A Labor Day celebration would be a good time for children to begin to learn more about their community and about career opportunities.

Scarry, Richard. **What Do People Do All Day?** Random House, 1968.

Many occupations are presented in this book about community helpers. Each page is full of illustrations and busy activities. Children will enjoy this book individually or with one other child because the illustrations are small and very detailed. Characters are animals dressed in job related uniforms. The use of this book should be accompanied by career information books and single stories on specific occupations.

Interviews. Interview children to find out what they would like to be. Or interview parents and other workers in the community to find out more about their jobs and what they do all day. Share interviews with the whole group. Use a tape recorder. (I,SG)

Twenty questions. Have each child think of a community helper. Allow the other children to ask up to twenty yes or no questions to see if they can guess the helper. The child to guess correctly will be the next one to be questioned. (SG,LG)

Field trips. Visit the work place of a parent or other selected community helper. Use children's literature as part of the preparation and follow-up for the field trip. (LG)

Programming notes: This is a good time to use the policeman/safety officer theme. Emphasis on safety rules including what to do about strangers, when you are home alone, or if you get lost are very appropriate for school-age children.

Ask the children which careers they would like to explore. Support the explorations with children's literature, resource persons, and field trips. Use props in dramatic play and block areas, as well as other centers and activities when appropriate, to encourage children to play out their concepts of the occupations presented.

GRANDPARENTS' DAY

Grandparents' Day is designated as the first Sunday in September after Labor Day. This is a special day school-age children will like to celebrate.

Wolf, Janet. **The Best Present Is Me.** Harper & Row, 1984.

On her weekly visit, a little girl has nothing to take to her grandmother but herself. Grandmother is so happy to see the little girl that her presence is the best gift of all. This story helps children realize that some of the best gifts do not cost money.

Grandparents' Day card. Use an 8½-by-11-inch sheet of paper folded in half for the card. Have children make their own decorations and designs on the outside and write a message on the inside. (I,SG)

Family tree. Have each child work on a simple family tree. Draw a simple tree. Write the child's name on the trunk. On the leaf area add the names of parents and grandparents. (I)

Grandparents' Day. Invite grandparents to visit. They might share brief stories about their childhood or special hobbies, talents, and interests. Grandparents might help children learn a special craft like crocheting, carving, or whittling, or stimulate a special interest. While grandparents are present have special refreshments. (LG)

96 / LET'S CELEBRATE

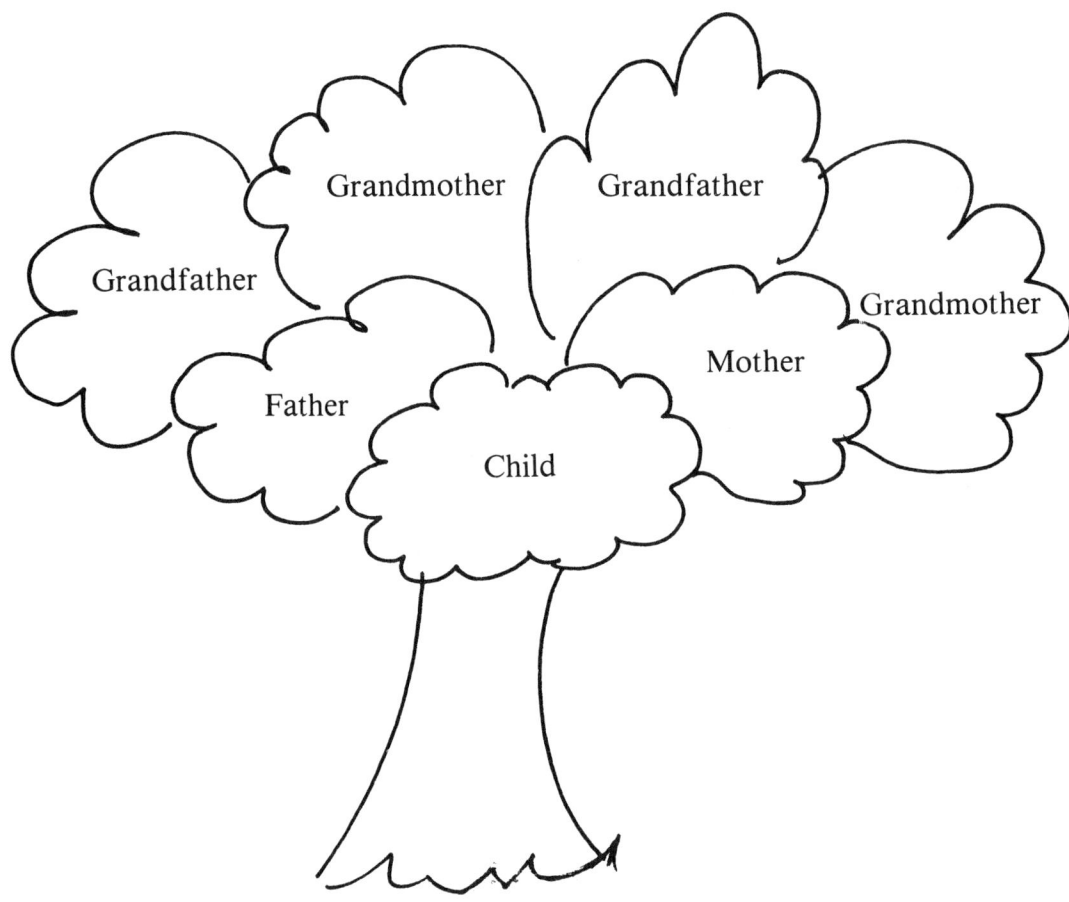

Visit a nursing or rest home. Make cards and plan special songs and other activities to share with residents of a nursing or rest home. The residents love to have company and this will be a special opportunity for children to share. (LG)

AMERICAN INDIAN DAY

American Indian or Native American Day is observed in most states on the fourth Friday of September. A unit on American Indians can stimulate a lot of interest in Indian crafts, foods, and customs.

Goble, Paul. **The Girl Who Loved Wild Horses.** Bradbury, 1978. Caldecott Medal Award.

A beautifully illustrated story of an Indian girl who loved wild horses. She was most happy when she was with the horses. Illustrations depict Indian life, costumes, and designs.

Indian arts and crafts. Use Indian arts and crafts ideas in the "Let's Create" chapter suggested for Gerald McDermott's *Arrow to the Sun*. Display arts and crafts projects.

Indian food. Cook Indian foods such as corn, popcorn, bread, and squash. Recipes for corn bread and Indian bread are found in the "Let's Cook" chapter for Aliki's *Corn Is Maize*. (SG,LG)

Alternate Indian titles:

Clark, Ann Nolan. *The Little Indian Basket Maker.* Illustrated by Harrison Begay. Melmont, 1957.

———. *The Little Indian Pottery Maker.* Illustrated by Don Perceval. Melmont, 1955.

Friskey, Margaret. *Indian Two Feet and His Eagle Feather.* Illustrated by John Hawkinson and Lucy O. Hawkinson. Children's Press, 1967.

Moon, Grace. *One Little Indian.* Whitman, 1967.

Programming notes: Learning about historical times is intriguing for school-age children. A theme on American Indian life is of special interest. To develop the theme more fully, add some of the ideas below.

- Display native American pictures depicting Indian life in early America.

- Display Indian costumes, pottery, arts, and crafts.

- Display an arrowhead collection.

- Visit an Indian museum.

- Invite a Native American to visit to share some of the history of his people.

- Make Indian drums and other musical instruments.

October

HALLOWEEN—October 31

Halloween is one of the oldest celebrations. It originated as a celebration of the eve of All Saints' Day thousands of years ago. This is one of the most festive, fun times for school-age children.

Bunting, Eve. **Scary, Scary Halloween.** Illustrated by Jan Brett. Clarion, 1986.

The story of how a mother cat and her kittens observe Halloween. The beautiful, realistic illustrations show children in the neighborhood trick-or-treating in their costumes on Halloween night. The illustrations give children and adults ideas for Halloween costumes and a variety of features for jack-o'-lanterns.

Jack-o'-lanterns. Identify the many different illustrations of jack-o'-lanterns in this title. Design original or copy some of the ideas for carving jack-o'-lanterns or for drawing or painting jack-o'-lanterns with a variety of features. (I,SG,LG)

Cavagnaro, David, and Maggie Cavagnaro. **The Pumpkin People.** Sierra Club Books, 1979.

A boy and his father share their pumpkin harvest with their neighbors. The celebration is just right for Halloween.

Pumpkin people. Have paper plates, orange tempera paint, and black or yellow construction paper. Paint paper plates orange. Let dry. Cut black or yellow jack-o'-lantern features out to glue on painted plates. Cut strips for arms and legs and staple to the sides and bottom of plate. Fold arms and legs accordian style and release. Hang with string in doorway or from the window for decorations. (SG,LG)

Field trip. Go to a pumpkin patch or an open air market. Select and purchase a pumpkin for a jack-o'-lantern. If possible, select more than one so several jack-o'-lanterns can be made. (LG)

Jack-o'-lantern. Carve a jack-o'-lantern. Save the seeds. For safety, use a small flashlight inside for light. Note: Have a jack-o'-lantern design contest. Encourage children to draw designs on paper first. Vote on the most popular design(s) to be used for the group jack-o'-lantern(s). (SG,LG)

Pumpkin cookies. Bake pumpkin cookies suggested in "Let's Cook" chapter for this title. Serve cookies for snack. Variation: Bake pumpkin pie or pumpkin bread. (SG)

Toasted pumpkin seeds. Follow the directions for toasted pumpkin seeds found in the "Let's Cook" chapter for this title.

Hoban, Lillian. **Arthur's Halloween Costume.** Harper & Row, 1984.

Arthur wants his costume for Halloween to be original. Most of the children are going to the school party as ghosts. Arthur wins the costume contest when he spills ketchup on his sheet and adds a wig and a few other items from a trash can to his costume.

Costume contest. Have children plan their own costume contest. Provide materials or ask children to bring materials they need for their costumes from home. Hint: Grocery bags make simple costumes. Cut holes for eyes and slits on the sides for shoulders and arms. Add features with markers, construction paper, yarn, felt, and fabric scraps. (LG)

Prelutsky, Jack. **It's Halloween.** Illustrated by Marilyn Hafner. Greenwillow, 1977.

A collection of thirteen funny and scary Halloween poems.

Scary stories. Make up scary stories to share with friends. Tell in a darkened room around the jack-o'-lantern or by flashlight under a table covered with a sheet or blanket.

Additional Halloween titles:

Adams, Adrienne. *A Woggle of Witches.* Scribner, 1971.

Alexander, Sue. *Witch, Goblin, and Ghost in the Haunted Woods.* Illustrated by Jeanette Winter. Pantheon Books, 1981.

Asch, Frank. *Popcorn.* Parent's Magazine Press, 1979.

Keats, Ezra Jack. *The Trip.* Greenwillow, 1978.

Kellogg, Steven. *The Mystery of the Flying Orange Pumpkin.* Dial, 1980.

Kraus, Robert. *How the Spiders Saved Halloween.* Dutton, 1973.

Low, Alice. *The Witch Who Was Afraid of Witches.* Illustrated by Karen Gundersheimer. Pantheon Books, 1978.

Roche, A. K. *The Pumpkin Heads.* Prentice-Hall, 1968.

Stevenson, James. *That Terrible Halloween Night.* Greenwillow, 1980.

Vigna, Judith. *Everybody Goes as a Pumpkin.* Whitman, 1977.

Watson, Jane Werner. *Which Is the Witch?* Illustrated by Victoria Dickerson Chess. Pantheon Books, 1979.

Zolotow, Charlotte. *A Tiger Called Thomas.* Illustrated by Kurt Werth. Lothrop, Lee and Shepard, 1963.

Programming notes: The ideas here may be too numerous to use all for a Halloween theme. Select the activities that will be the most enjoyable for your group. Ideas for spiders and monsters should also be considered for the Halloween theme.

November

THANKSGIVING

Thanksgiving Day is observed on the fourth Thursday of November. The original Thanksgiving was observed by the Pilgrims with their new found friends, the Indians. They celebrated the fall harvest with a feast after a year of hardship in America. Abraham Lincoln designated the fourth Thursday in November as the national day of Thanksgiving when he was president. Thanksgiving is a time for family and friends to be together and to celebrate with a feast including turkey, cranberry sauce, yams, and pumpkin pie.

Child, Lydia Maria. **Over the River and Through the Wood.** Illustrated by Brinton Turkle. Coward, McCann, and Geoghegan, 1974.

The traditional Thanksgiving song with illustrations from the horse and sleigh period. Appealing illustrations to accompany the words of the song.

Song. Use this song as the theme song. Learn the song for group singing. Use jingle bells or sleigh bells to accompany the singing of the song. Note: See the description of jingle bells for Lydia Maria Child's *Over the River and Through the Wood* in the "Let's Make Music" chapter. (LG)

Devlin, Wende, and Harry Devlin. **Cranberry Thanksgiving.** Parent's Magazine Press, 1971.

Maggie invites a special guest to Thanksgiving dinner. One of the special treats is grandmother's cranberry bread. The recipe for cranberry bread is in the book.

Cranberry bread. Bake cranberry bread using the recipe in the book. Note: A cranberry bread mix can be found at the grocery store. (SG,LG)

Cranberry relish. Make cranberry relish as gifts at Thanksgiving. The relish recipe is in "Let's Cook" chapter where it is suggested as an activity for *Cranberry Thanksgiving.* (SG)

100 / LET'S CELEBRATE

Programming notes: Consider the additional activities suggested below for the Thanksgiving theme.

- Make vegetable soup. Have each child bring a vegetable to add to the soup. The recipe for stone soup in Marcia Brown's *Stone Soup* in the chapter "Let's Cook," without the stones, makes delicious vegetable soup.

- Have a Thanksgiving feast. Have Indians and Pilgrims. Make hats for Pilgrims and head bands for Indians.

- For a bulletin board display, have children draw or paint pictures for things for which they are thankful.

December

CHRISTMAS

Christmas Day, December 25, is the day we celebrate the birth of Jesus Christ. The Christmas season covers a span of time before and after this day. School-age children may be actively involved in the celebration of Christmas, a special time of giving and sharing.

De Paola, Tomie. **The Christmas Pageant.** Winston, 1981.
    The Christmas story with cut out puppets to color and assemble for a Christmas pageant. The small size of the cut outs are more appropriate for school-age children than preschoolers.
    Puppet show. Use the cut outs for stick puppets for a puppet show. Directions for a puppet show are presented in the book. (I,SG)

De Paola, Tomie. **The Story of the Three Wise Kings.** Putnam's Sons, 1983.
    A colorful account of the three wise men who went to Bethlehem to see Jesus. Simply told, beautifully illustrated, and easily dramatized.
    Dramatize the story. See dramatization suggestions in this chapter for Three Kings' Day, January 6. (SG)

Ets, Marie Hall. **Nine Days to Christmas.** Viking, 1959. Caldecott Medal Award.
    A story of a Mexican Christmas and the search for the right pinata. The pictures capture the preparation and celebration of the Christmas season as five-year-old Ceci plans her own posada—parties held on the nine days before Christmas.
    Piñata. Have available grocery bags, newspaper, wrapped candies, yarn, streamers, paints or felt tipped markers. Stuff a paper bag with newspapers and candies. Tie at the top. Decorate with streamers, paints, or whatever you desire. Hang with a sturdy string. Take turns hitting the piñata with a stick until it breaks. Enjoy the treats. This can be a group project. Note: This is a very simple piñata. Make one as fancy as you wish. (SG,LG)
    God's eye. God's eyes were originally used by Mexican Indians in their dwellings as symbols of God's care and protection. They are also used for ornamentation and decoration. God's eyes in Christmas colors or white and gold make very pretty Christmas tree ornaments. Use 6-inch sticks (small dowel sticks) and colorful, or white and gold yarn. (1) Make a cross of two sticks and tie them together with yarn. (2) Circle the sticks with the yarn. Change colors by tying new yarn on to the end of the original color. (3) When the God's eye is complete, add tassels on the stick ends. (I,SG)

Children's Literature and Special Days of the Year / 101

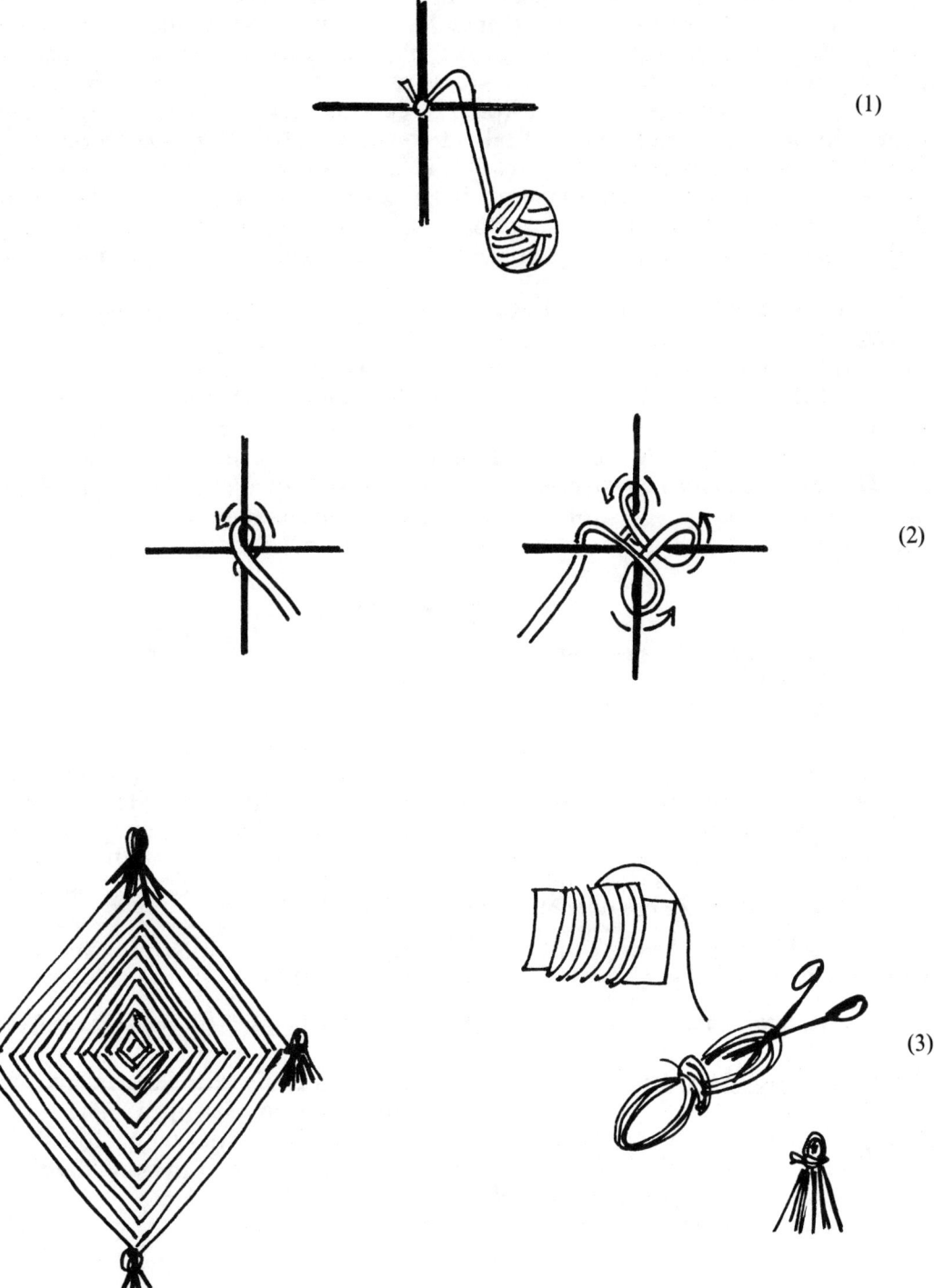

(1)

(2)

(3)

102 / LET'S CELEBRATE

Hoban, Lillian. **Arthur's Christmas Cookies.** Harper & Row, 1972.

Arthur, a chimpanzee, has no money for presents so he decides to make cookies for his family. He uses salt instead of sugar so his cookies are different. They cannot be eaten but make perfect new Christmas tree ornaments—presents members of his family can enjoy and keep.

Play-clay ornaments. Use 4 cups flour, 1 cup salt, and 1½ cups water. Mix ingredients together. Knead dough until smooth. Roll out dough to a ½-inch thick sheet on waxed paper. Use Christmas cookie cutters to cut out cookie shaped ornaments. Place on cookie sheet. Make a hole at the top of each dough ornament. Bake at 300 degrees for an hour. When cold, paint and decorate. Paint with acrylic paints or spray with a fixative or shellac if tempera paint is used. String a piece of yarn through the hole and tie ends together to serve as a hanger. (I,SG)

Holmes, Efner Tudor. **The Christmas Cat.** Illustrated by Tasha Tudor. Crowell, 1976.

A lost cat was brought to two brothers, Nate and Jason, by their father on Christmas Eve. The brothers participated with their family in several Christmas traditions. They baked and decorated gingerbread animal cookies for the Christmas tree, listened to father read "The Night Before Christmas," and lit candles in front of the crèche. The recipes for gingerbread animal cookies and white frosting are included on the back page of the book.

Gingerbread animal cookies. Have available a variety of animal cookie cutters. Use the recipe in the book to make cookies for Christmas tree ornaments. Use the frosting recipe in the book for decorating the cookies or use the following less complicated recipe.

White Icing

1 pound confectioners sugar
3 egg whites
1 tablespoon white vinegar

Place sugar in mixing bowl. Beat egg whites slightly with a fork. Add to sugar and beat with an electric mixer on lowest speed for one minute. Add vinegar and beat two minutes more at high speed, or until stiff and glossy. Apply to cookie with a pastry tube. If a pastry tube is not available, make a cone from a piece of strong brown or waxed paper. Secure on the side with a pin or a toothpick. Squeeze frosting through the small opening at the point of the cone. Cut point to make opening as large as needed. (I,SG)

Read "The Night Before Christmas." Read aloud "The Night Before Christmas." Have different versions available for children to view and read. (I,SG,LG)

Programming notes: The gingerbread cookies may be used for snack or refreshments.

Menotti, Gian Carlo. **Amahl and the Night Visitors.** Illustrated by Michéle Lemieux. Morrow, 1986.

Beautifully illustrated adaptation of Carlo Menotti's popular opera. The story of the three wise men's visit with a poor, lame boy as they look for Jesus, Mary, and Joseph.

Amahl and the Night Visitors. Arrange to see a production of this popular Christmas story, or secure and view a video recording of the opera. (SG,LG)

Read the story and listen to a recording. Read the story aloud to the group. Follow the reading of the story with listening to a recording of the opera. Compare the two. Did the recording contain all of the story?

Programming notes: Use this title along with other titles of the birth of Jesus. *Amahl and the Night Visitors* is an enjoyable introduction to opera for children. (I,SG,LG)

The Twelve Days of Christmas. Illustrated by Jan Brett. Dodd, Mead & Co., 1986.

A traditional Christmas carol used originally as a counting song and children's parlor game. A beautifully illustrated edition. Each illustration is bordered with traditional Christmas folk motifs, a family's preparation for Christmas, and "Merry Christmas" written in eleven different languages. The editor's notes give the history of the carol and its original uses.

Game song. Play a game using the song, as was the custom in the late 1700s. Seat the group in a circle. The leader of the game begins by singing the lines for the first day. Everyone in the circle is to repeat the lines in turn. Then the first lines are repeated by the leader and the lines for the second day are added. Again, in turn, everyone in the circle repeats all that the leader sings. Continue until all the lines for the twelve days are repeated by everyone. If anyone misses a line, he or she must give something to the group or may choose to drop out of the game. (SG,LG)

Merry Christmas. Find "Merry Christmas" written in eleven languages. List each one on a sheet of paper or poster board. Identify and write the language beside each "Merry Christmas." Learn to say "Merry Christmas" in the eleven languages. (I,SG)

Wilson, Robina B. **Merry Christmas: Children at Christmastime Around the World.** Illustrated by Satomi Ichikawa. Putnam's Sons, 1983.

A book for children which depicts how children around the world celebrate Christmas. Starting with the nativity story, the book included information about Christmas customs, legends, carols, and instructions for making decorations and cakes for several countries around the world.

International Christmas. After sharing this book with the children, let them help select decorations, activities, and cooking projects they would like to make and do to celebrate Christmas as other children around the world do. Children might be directed to select a country and participate in a variety of activities for several days. Different groups may choose different countries or the whole group might participate in activities from a single country for a shorter period of time. (SG,LG)

Programming notes: An international Christmas theme can be developed even if Wilson's book is not available. Select Christmas stories from other countries and find facts about each country's customs. A good start are the suggestions for Marie Hall Ets's *Nine Days of Christmas*, a Mexican Christmas.

Additional Christmas titles:

De Paola, Tomie. *The Clown of God: An Old Story.* Harcourt, Brace, Jovanovich, 1978.

Kelley, Emily. *Christmas Around the World: A Celebration.* Illustrated by Priscilla Kiedrowski. Carolrhoda, 1985.

Moore, Clement Clarke. *The Night Before Christmas.* Illustrated by Tasha Tudor. Rand McNally, 1975.

_____ . *A Visit from St. Nicholas: 'Twas the Night Before Christmas.* Illustrated by Paul Galdone. McGraw-Hill, 1968.

Spier, Peter. *Peter Spier's Christmas.* Doubleday, 1983.

Thomas, Dylan. *A Child's Christmas in Wales.* Illustrated by Trina Schart Hyman. Holiday House, 1985.

Van Allsburg, Chris. *The Polar Express.* Houghton-Mifflin, 1985.

We Wish You a Merry Christmas. Illustrated by Tracey Campbell Pearson. Dial, 1983. (A single song picture book of the traditional Christmas carol.)

104 / LET'S CELEBRATE

Programming notes: Children will be involved in Christmas celebrations at home, at school, and in their child care program. A special emphasis for the child care program might be that of giving and sharing with others. Plan to involve parents, too. Some giving and sharing activities are listed below. Encourage children to make and plan additional activities.

- Learn Christmas carols and songs. Sing as a group. Plan to go caroling.

- Make Christmas sugar cookies. See butter cookie recipe in "Let's Cook" for St. Patrick's Day.

- Visit a shut-in or nursing home. Sing Christmas songs, act out Christmas stories, and share Christmas cookies, cards, and decorations.

- Make a variety of Christmas cards and decorations.

- Collect and repair toys to give as gifts to needy children. Contribute the toys to the community group distributing toys for the needy.

HANUKKAH

Hanukkah is the Jewish Festival of Lights. It is a Jewish holiday celebrated for eight days, normally in December, determined by the lunar calendar. Families have parties, gifts are exchanged, and children are given dreidels or little spinning tops for games. During Hanukkah, candles on the nine-branched menorah are lit, one each day, in thanksgiving for the early Jews' freedom from religious oppression.

Fisher, Aileen. **My First Hanukkah Book.** Illustrated by Priscilla Kiedrowski. Children's Press, 1985.
　　Poems for children exploring various aspects of Hanukkah—its historical significance, symbols, family celebrations, treats, and games. Full color illustrations face each poem.

Hirsh, Marilyn. **I Love Hanukkah.** Holiday House, 1984.
　　Grandfather tells his young grandson the story of Hanukkah and the meaning of the eight-day celebration. The illustrations are very interesting, with the ancient Hanukkah story drawn on a small scale while present day scenes are illustrated in larger, bold drawings.
　　Dreidel. Buy a commercially made dreidel or make a simple one from cardboard and a pencil. To make a cardboard and pencil dreidel, cut a 3-inch square of cardboard. Draw lines from corner to corner, crossing in the middle. In each section write one of the following: "Take 1," "Return 1," "Take All," "Return All." Carefully make a hole in the center of the cardboard square where the lines cross. Place a pencil in this hole in the center of the cardboard square, working it down until it spins easily. The point should be rounded, not too sharp. Note: An authentic dreidel has Hebrew letters on each side that stand for Yiddish words for take, nothing, half, and return. An adaptation is suggested here because using the real dreidel symbols to play a dreidel game might be too hard for most young children. Older children will find a version of the authentic dreidel game challenging.[3] (I,SG)

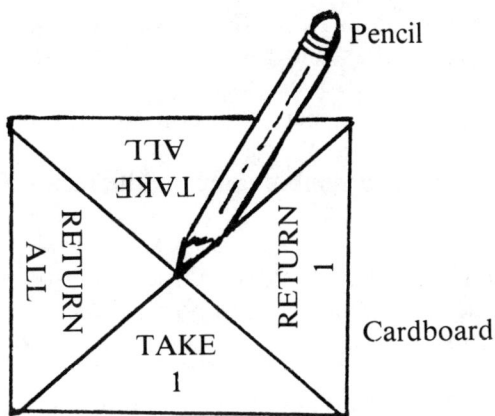

Dreidel game. To play a simple dreidel game, provide dried kidney beans and a dreidel with "Take 1," "Return 1," "Take All," and "Return All" written on the sides of the dreidel. Place 20 beans in a saucer from which to take or return. Give each player 4 beans to start. Players take turns spinning the dreidel and responding to the directions on the side of the dreidel when it stops spinning and falls over on its side. The winner is the player who has the most beans when the game ends. (SG)

Dreidel song. Sing the dreidel song. The song can be found in song books for children. The first verse is as follows:

Oh, dreidel, dreidel, dreidel,
I made it out of clay.
And when my dreidel's ready,
Oh, dreidel I will play!

Children enjoy singing the song as they spin their dreidels. (I,SG,LG)

Additional Hanukkah titles:

Adler, David A. *A Picture Book of Hanukkah.* Holiday House, 1982.

Aleichem, Sholom. *Hanukah Money.* Illustrated by Uri Shulevitz. Greenwillow, 1978.

Coopersmith, Jerome. *A Chanukah Fable for Christmas.* Illustrated by Syd Hoff. Putnam's Sons, 1969.

Simon, Norma. *Hanukkah.* Illustrated by Symeon Shimin. Crowell, 1966.

Programming notes: Include some of the following additional activities to celebrate Hanukkah:

- Make potato pancakes as suggested in the "Let's Cook" chapter for Sholom Aleichem's *Hanukah Money.*

- Visit a Jewish synagogue.

- Find out facts about the Jewish faith.

- Have a rabbi or another adult from the Jewish faith visit to share with the children firsthand information about Hanukkah and the customs related to this celebration.

- Make a menorah picture or poster from construction paper.

- Make Hanukkah cards. Use symbols such as the menorah, Star of David, candle, or dreidel for the front of the card.

- Make a Star of David from craft sticks. Glue three sticks in the shape of a triangle. Repeat. Place triangles on top of each other in opposite directions. The shape will look like the Star of David with six points.

- Make sugar cookies for the Hanukkah celebration. Use candle and Star of David shapes to cut out cookies or use dough to make the shapes of the Hebrew letters found on a dreidel.

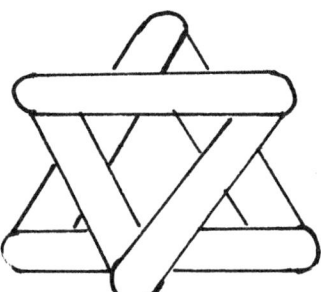

NOTES

[1] Ruth White and Alexandra Kusion-Rowe, *Happy Holidays: Activities for Fun and Learning* (Los Angeles, Calif.: Rhythms Publications, 1980), 37.

[2] White and Kusion-Rowe, *Happy Holidays*, 37.

[3] Marilyn Burns, *The Hanukkah Book*, illus. Martha Weston (New York: Four Winds, 1981), 73-76.

7
RESOURCES
A Selected Annotated Bibliography

The following bibliography includes children's literature related sources, selection tools for children's literature, activity resources, and periodicals useful for teachers in planning literature related activities for kindergarten through third grade.

GENERAL

Bauer, Caroline Feller. **Celebrations.** New York: Wilson, 1985.
   Holiday and theme book programs to be read aloud. A collection of sixteen book programs based on holidays, events, and choice other topics. Prose, poetry, and a variety of activities are offered.

_____ . **Handbook for Storytellers.** Chicago: American Library Association, 1977.
   A guide to planning and implementing storytelling programs describing a variety of methods for storytelling. Especially good resource for puppetry and music.

_____ . **This Way to Books.** New York: Wilson, 1983.
   For librarians, teachers, and parents. Hundreds of ideas and programs designed to get children and books together. Full of useful information, tips, and suggestions. The book is divided into the following sections: storytelling, programs, booktalks, poetry, games, crafts, and exhibits.

Borba, Michele, and Dan Ungaro. **Bookends.** Carthage, Ill.: Good Apple, 1982.
   Numerous ideas for primary-age children to enhance their experience with their literature. Excellent suggestions for activities, book centers, and a variety of creative and research experiences. Good resource for unit or theme planning.

Cianciolo, Patricia Jean. **Picture Books for Children.** 2nd ed. Chicago: American Library Association, 1981.
   Excellent reference book on illustrators and their illustrations. Especially good when studying specific illustrators and their distinctive illustration techniques.

Commire, Anne, ed. **Something about the Author: Facts and Pictures About Authors and Illustrators of Books for Young People.** Detroit: Gale Research, 1980.
   Biographical sketches of nearly 57,000 authors of children's books. Useful for children who become intrigued with an author.

Cullinan, Bernice E. **Literature and the Child.** New York: Harcourt, Brace, Jovanovich, 1981.
   A textbook for students of children's literature. Many ideas for helping children relate to their literature are given.

Good News Bible. New York: American Bible Society, 1976.
   The Bible in "Today's English Version," a modern translation easier for children to read and understand. The purpose of this translation is to present clearly and accurately the meaning of the original text for people whose primary language is English.

Graham, Terry. **Let Loose on Mother Goose.** Nashville, Tenn.: Incentive Publications, 1982.
   A resource suggesting activities based on nursery rhymes to teach math, science, art, music, life skills, and language development.

Huck, Charlotte S. **Children's Literature in the Elementary School.** 3rd ed. New York: Holt, Rinehart and Winston, 1979.
   Children's literature text with an excellent chapter on extending the literature through activities.

Lamme, Linda Leonard, ed. **Learning to Love Literature: Preschool Through Grade 3.** Urbana, Ill.: National Council of Teachers of English, 1981.
   An excellent guide for early childhood teachers and librarians suggesting ways to integrate children's literature into the curricula. Children's literature titles and appropriate curricula areas are given.

Lewis, Marguerite. **Hooked on Reading!** West Nyack, N.Y.: Center for Applied Research in Education, 1986.
   A unique resource for school librarians, classroom teachers, and reading specialists in second through eighth grades provides 114 reproducible wordsearch and crossword puzzles to encourage students to read and enjoy Newbery and Caldecott Award Winners.

Norton, Donna E. **Through the Eyes of a Child: An Introduction to Children's Literature.** Columbus, Ohio: Merrill, 1983.
   Extremely useful children's literature text with many ideas for extending children's experiences with their literature.

Paulin, Mary Ann. **Creative Uses of Children's Literature.** Hamden, Conn.: Library Professional Publications, 1982.
   Thousands of ideas for using books with young people.

Pearl, Patricia, comp. **Religious Books for Children: An Annotated Bibliography.** Bryn Mawr, Penn.: Church and Synagogue Library Association, 1983.
   An annotated bibliography of children's religious books. Exceptional or particularly important books in their categories are starred.

Polette, Nancy. **E Is for Everybody.** 2nd ed. Metuchen, N.J.: Scarecrow, 1982.
   A manual including activities in creative dramatics, art, writing, and games related to 126 children's easy titles.

Somers, Albert B., and Janet Evans Worthington. **Response Guides for Teaching Children's Books.** Urbana, Ill.: National Council of Teachers of English, 1979.
   A resource guide for teaching children's books. Includes a variety of suggestions for extending a child's experiences with twenty-seven selected titles.

Sutherland, Zena, Dianne L. Monson, and Mary Hill Arbuthnot. **Children and Books.** 6th ed. Glenview, Ill.: Scott Foresman, 1981.
    Children's literature text with good information on picture books.

Trelease, Jim. **The Read-Aloud Handbook.** New York: Penguin, 1985.
    A guide for parents and teachers to more than 300 great read-aloud books for children.

Wendelin, Karla Hawkins, and M. Jean Greenlaw. **Storybook Classroom: Using Children's Literature in the Learning Center.** Atlanta, Ga.: Humanics Limited, 1984.
    A resource for the media center or classroom. Presents many ideas for extending a child's experience with literature and instructions on how to set up learning centers.

White, Ruth, and Alexandra Kusion-Rowe. **Happy Holidays: Activities for Fun and Learning.** Los Angeles, Calif.: Rhythms Productions, 1980.
    A useful book of ideas for holidays arranged by the month. Ideas for activities children can easily participate in including music and art.

SELECTION TOOLS FOR CHILDREN'S LITERATURE

Isaacson, Richard H., Ferne E. Hillegas, and Juliette Yaakov, eds. **Children's Catalog.** 15th ed. New York: Wilson, 1986.
    An annotated bibliography of selected print materials for children, with titles arranged by Dewey Decimal Classification.

Lima, Carolyn W. **A to Zoo: Subject Access to Children's Picture Books.** 2nd ed. New York: Bowker, 1985.
    A subject guide index to picture books. A useful resource for unit planning.

Pearl, Patricia, comp. **Religious Books for Children: An Annotated Bibliography.** Bryn Mawr, Penn.: Church and Synagogue Library Association, 1983.
    An annotated bibliography of religious books for children with the best books in each category starred.

White, Mary Lou, ed. **Adventuring with Books.** New ed. Urbana, Ill.: National Council of Teachers of English, 1985.
    A selective booklist designed for teachers of preschool through sixth grade children. Arranged by categories and subjects. Each entry is annotated.

Winkel, Lois, ed. **The Elementary School Library Collection.** 15th ed. Williamsport, Penn.: Brodart, 1986.
    A bibliography of children's literature including print and nonprint materials. An excellent selection tool.

PERIODICALS

Child Care Exchange. Redmond, Wash.: Child Care Exchange.
    The director's magazine with an abundance of administrative helps.

Day Care and Early Education. New York: Humanics Press.
    Ideas from administration to curriculum. Special articles are often included on curriculum areas and school-age child care.

110 / RESOURCES

Early Years. Darien, Conn.: Allen Raymond, Inc.
    Periodical for preschool and primary teachers. Contains a monthly section on children's literature.

First Teacher. Bridgeport, Conn.: First Teacher, Inc.
    Packed full of programming and curriculum ideas. A monthly section for preschoolers. Many ideas may be adapted by older children.

Highlights for Children. Columbus, Ohio: Highlights, Inc.
    A monthly periodical for children full of stories and learning activities. Especially good resource for holiday and special occasion ideas.

Instructor and Teacher Magazine. Duluth, Minn.: Instructor Publications, Inc.
    Planning and curriculum ideas for teachers.

School Age Notes. Nashville, Tenn.: School-Age Notes, Inc.
    A newsletter for after-school programs. A must for teachers and directors. Includes ideas from administration to programming. Special listings in each issue of selected and reviewed resources for school-age child care teachers very valuable.

SCHOOL-AGE CHILD CARE ADMINISTRATION AND PROGRAMMING

"Administrative Notes: School Facilities Child Care Act." **School Age Notes** 4 (January/February 1984): 10.
    A summary of the School Facilities Child Care Act (Senate Bill S1531). Includes findings of the study committee on the need for school-age child care and the resulting recommendations of the committee. Use of public school facilities for before and after school hours for the care of school-age children is encouraged.

Alexander, Nancy P. "School-Age Child Care: Concerns and Challenges." **Young Children** 42 (November 1986): 3-10.
    A summary of the needs for and components of good school-age child care. The need for adequate supervision for all school-age children is stressed and program alternatives are suggested.

Baden, Ruth, Andrea Genser, James Levine, and Michelle Seligson. **School-Age Child Care: An Action Manual.** Boston: Auburn House, 1982.
    Written for groups interested in organizing school-age care. No activities suggested but does address starting and managing programs including curriculum development, budgeting, personnel issues, policy-making, and much more.

Bender, Judith, Charles Flatter, and Barbara Schuyler-Haas Elder. **Half a Childhood: Time for School-Age Child Care.** Nashville, Tenn.: School-Age Notes, Inc. 1984.
    Provides practical information on the need for school-age child care. Activities suggestions for programming are suggested.

Bergstrom, Joan. **School's Out—Now What?** Berkeley, Calif.: Ten Speed, 1984.
    Provides parents with suggestions for creative choices for their children's out-of-school hours. Presents developmental information and covers TV, reading, chores, homework, activities, and much more. Resources for parents and school-age children extremely valuable.

Blau, Rosalie, Elizabeth H. Brady, Ida Bucher, Betsy Hiteshaw, Ann Zavitkovsky, and Docia Zavitkovsky. **Activities for School-Age Child Care.** Washington, D.C.: National Association for the Education of Young Children, 1977.

Ideas for program planning including arts and crafts, music and dance, puppets, dramatic play, cooking, science, and more. Resource for scheduling, routines, community resources, and staff meetings.

Browne, Gayle, ed. **Day Care for School-Agers.** Austin, Tex.: Texas Department of Human Resources, 1977.

A large, loose-leaf book full of good program ideas, useful bibliographies, activity suggestions, equipment, management tips, and environmental designs.

Cohen, Abby J. **School-Age Child Care: A Legal Manual for Public School Administrators.** Wellesley, Mass.: School-Age Child Care Project, 1984.

A manual for public school providers of extended-day or school-based programs in public schools.

Cohen, Donald J., Ronald K. Parker, Malcolm S. Host, and Catherine Richards, eds. **Day Care: Serving School-Age Children.** Washington, D.C.: U.S. Department of Health, Education and Welfare, 1972.

Provides both child development information and program ideas for school-age children. Contains a useful list of resources and publications on school-age child care. Available from Superintendent of Documents, U.S. Government Printing Office, Washington, D.C. 20402.

Coolsen, Peter, Michelle Seligson, and James Garbarino. **When School's Out and Nobody's Home.** Chicago: National Committee for Prevention of Child Abuse, 1985.

Latchkey problems and concerns as well as suggested options for parents and their children are given.

Erikson, Erik H. **Childhood and Society.** 2nd ed. New York: Norton, 1963.

A detailed account of Erikson's theory of child development. Important background knowledge for planning developmentally appropriate programs for children.

Evette, Leita. "Ministry Through Before- and After-School Care." **Church Administration** 26 (December 1983): 17-19.

Avenues of ministry and elements of quality child care are presented. Directed specifically to churches responding to the needs of school-age children and their parents in communities where child care needs exist.

Gesell, Arnold, Frances L. Ilg, and Louise Bates Ames. **The Child from Five to Ten.** Rev. ed. New York: Harper & Row, 1977.

A very easy to understand child development text. Characteristics and suggestions for guidance at each chronological age and stages of development are given. Helpful resource for teachers and parents.

Ilg, Frances L., Louise Bates Ames, and Sidney M. Baker. **Child Behavior.** New York: Harper & Row, 1981.

Developmental characteristics and expectations of children at stages of development from birth through the beginning school years are given. Guidance techniques and narrative concerning child behavior provide a resource for better understanding children, their needs, and their behavior.

112 / RESOURCES

Long, Lynette, and Thomas Long. **The Handbook for Latchkey Children and Their Parents.** New York: Arbor House, 1983.
    A review of the prevalence of latchkey children and the problems and concerns this situation causes for parents and their children. A good review of child care programs that work for children and suggestions for parents are important elements in this book.

McNairy, Marion R. "School-Age Child Care: Program and Policy Issues." **Educational Horizons** 62 (Winter 1984): 64-67.
    Who responds to the growing need for school-age child care? The interrelationships of the role of educators in partnership with other groups concerned about program and policy issues in school-age child care programs are presented.

Military Child Care Project, Department of Defense. **Caring for School-Age Children.** Washington, D.C.: U.S. Government Printing Office, 1982.
    A training module for school-age child care teachers dealing with school-age children's developmental needs. Provides appropriate programming and individual and group management techniques. Part of the Military Child Care Project Staff Development Series.

_____ . **Creating Environments for School-Age Child Care.** Washington, D.C.: U.S. Government Printing Office, 1982.
    Developed as a training manual, presents ways to plan the physical space and ways to use people and things. Suggestions are made to help children become independent and creative. Valuable resource for environment and activity planning. Part of the Military Child Care Project Child Environment Series.

Neugebauer, Roger. "School Age Day Care Reprint," **Child Care Information Exchange.** Redmond, Wash.: 1980.
    Comprehensive summary of the needs and steps in organizing a school-age child care program.

Nieting, Peggy Lewis. "School-Age Child Care: In Support of Development and Learning." **Childhood Education** 60 (September/October 1983): 6-11.
    School-age child care is defined, the requirements presented, and components of a responsive program discussed. The roles of the family, school, and community in such programming are presented.

Prescott, Elizabeth, and Cynthia Milich. **School's Out! Group Day Care for the School-Age Child.** Pasadena, Calif.: Pacific Oaks, 1974.
    Resource for directors and program planners. Helpful for those responsible for establishing and evaluating the total school-age program.

Schofield, Richard T., and Jean Watson Shaw. "Programming for School-Age Children in Child Care." **Day Care and Early Education** 8 (Spring 1981): 19-22.
    A well-defined purpose and philosophy based on the changing needs of the children, parents, program, and community is a must for good school-age child care programs. Different approaches to programming are presented, with emphasis on an educational programming that does not duplicate but supplements the school and supports the home.

School-Age Child Care. Champaign, Ill.: YMCA, 1982.
    Programming manual for the YMCA school-age child care programs. Available from YMCA Program Store, Box 5077, Champaign, Ill. 61820.

Sciarra, Dorothy June, and Anne G. Dorsey. **Developing and Administering a Child Care Center.** Boston: Houghton-Mifflin, 1979.

    A general administrative guide for child care center directors. Helpful aids in developing program policies and administrative procedures.

ART ACTIVITIES

Art: A Creative Curriculum for Early Childhood. Washington, D.C.: Creative Associates, 1979.

    A useful resource on techniques for creative art activities.

Bernstein, Bonnie, and Leigh Blair. **Native American Crafts Workshop Series.** Belmont, Calif.: Pitman, 1982.

    A crafts workshop series appropriate for school-age children. The series includes *Native American Crafts, Trash Artists, Nature Crafts, Writing Crafts,* and *Make Your Own Games.*

Caballero, Jane, and Derek Whordley. **Children Around the World.** Atlanta, Ga.: Humanics Limited, 1983.

    A resource of factual information and customs of various cultures around the world. Includes suggested activities, games, crafts, and recipes for each country. A bibliography for children for more in-depth study of each country is presented.

Fiarotta, Phyllis. **Sticks and Stones and Ice Cream Cones: The Craft Book for Children.** New York: Workman, 1973.

    A basic crafts reference for children. Easy directions and diagrams for children to follow.

Forte, Imogene. **Arts and Crafts: From Things Around the House.** Nashville, Tenn.: Incentive Publications, 1983.

    Arts and crafts ideas for home or school. Suggestions for recycling materials around the house are an asset to program with limited budget.

Frank, Marjorie. **I Can Make a Rainbow.** Nashville, Tenn.: Incentive Publications, 1976.

    Things to create and do for children and adults. Includes art, cooking, and many other ideas. Directions can easily be understood by beginning readers.

Hawkinson, John. **A Ball of Clay.** Chicago: Whitman, 1974.

    Factual information about clay and clay art. Techniques and ideas are presented for a variety of activities with clay.

Instructor's Artfully Easy! New York: Instructor Publications, 1983.

    A collection of art ideas that previously appeared in the *Instructor* and the *Instructor and Teacher Magazine* from 1975 to 1983. Excellent ideas with simple instructions and actual photographs of finished artistic creations.

Instructor's Big Seasonal Art and Crafts Book. New York: Instructor Publications, 1979.

    Simple instructions and actual photographs of the finished product for art activities in categories of fall, winter, spring, summer, and any time.

Lamme, Linda Leonard, and Francis Kane. "Children, Books, and Collage." **Language Arts** 53 (November/December 1976): 902-05.

    An interesting article on illustrators who use collage and some of their work.

114 / RESOURCES

Petrich, Patricia, and Rosemary Dalton. **The Kids Arts and Crafts Book.** Concord, Calif.: Nitty Gritty Publications, 1975.
    A collection of arts and craft ideas for young children. Techniques, simple directions, and illustrations of children's actual art work are given.

Romberg, Jenean. **Let's Discover Art Series.** West Nyack, N.Y.: Center for Applied Research in Education, 1973-1976.
    An excellent art activity resource for school-age children. Each book presents techniques for specific medium and suggests activities ranging from easy to hard. The series includes *Let's Discover Crayon, Mobiles, Puppets, Watercolor, Tempera,* and *Tissue.*

Temko, Florence. **Folk Crafts for World Friendship.** Illustrated by Yaroslava. Garden City, N.Y.: Doubleday, 1976.
    Customs and arts and craft ideas from many countries around the world. Young children can do most of the activities.

Warren, Jean. **Crafts.** Illustrated by Susan True. Palo Alto, Calif.: Monday Morning Books, 1983.
    A collection of creative art activities for young children. Includes some seasonal ideas and some different ways to use familiar art materials.

Wiseman, Ann. **Making Things: The Hand Book of Creative Discovery.** Boston: Little, Brown, & Co., 1973.
    Ideas for unique, creative art activities for school-age children. Art suggestions are especially appropriate for older children. Real tools and materials are required. Activities allow for creativity within the directions for a specific finished product.

CREATIVE DRAMATICS

Bauer, Caroline Feller. **Handbook for Storytellers.** Chicago: American Library Association, 1977.
    Resource for teachers presenting ideas for storytelling and much more for sharing literature with children. Good chapter on puppets.

Cottrell, June. **Teaching with Creative Dramatics.** Skokie, Ill.: National Textbook Co., 1975.
    A textbook approach to creative dramatics. Background information, techniques, and examples are presented.

Gillies, Emily. **Creative Dramatics for All Children.** Washington, D.C.: National Association for the Education of Young Children, 1973.
    A good resource for teachers beginning creative dramatics with children. Includes techniques and resource list.

Williamson, P.M. "Literature Goals and Activities for Young Children." **Young Children** 36 (May 1981): 24-30.
    A useful article on the value of the use of literature related activities with children. Creative dramatic activities specifically highlighted.

Zinmaster, Wanna. "Dramatizing Literature with Young Children." In Leland B. Jacobs, ed. **Using Literature with Young Children.** New York: Teachers College Press, 1965.
    One of several articles on creative responses to children's literature. A useful handbook on techniques and a variety of ways to respond to literature.

MUSIC

Butler, Theodore, ed. **Music for Today's Children.** Nashville, Tenn.: Broadman, 1975.
    An excellent collection of children's songs including many songs that never grow old.

Hawkinson, John, and Martha Faulhaber. **Music and Instruments for Children to Make.** Chicago: Whitman, 1970.
    A resource for teachers and parents dealing with basic rhythms and music in young children's lives. Instructions for simple instruments are included.

Johns, Timothy, and Peter Hankey, eds. **The Great Song Book.** Illustrated by Tomi Ungerer. Garden City, N.Y.: Doubleday, 1978.
    A collection of well-known traditional songs and some less-known songs. Includes a range of songs from dance and play to nursery rhymes. The full-color illustrations enhance the book.

Lamme, Linda Leonard. "Song Picture Books—A Maturing Genre of Children's Literature." **Language Arts** 56 (April 1979): 400-07.
    Identifies many single song picture books and makes comparisons of the same titles by different authors. The best single song picture books are indicated.

McDonald, Dorothy L. **Music In Our Lives: The Early Years.** Washington, D.C.: National Association for the Education of Young Children, 1979.
    A book about children, teachers, and their music in early childhood programs. Techniques and development of music skills.

Ramsey, Bayless. **Music: A Way of Life for the Young Child.** 2nd ed. St. Louis, Mo.: Mosby Co., 1982.
    Useful suggestions for use of music with young children. Section on homemade instruments especially good.

Walther, Tom. **Make Mine Music!** Boston: Little, Brown, & Co., 1981.
    A variety of musical instruments are discussed and directions for making and playing them are given. Directions for making African instruments most useful.

COOKING

Ackerman, Caroline. **Cooking with Kids.** Mt. Rainer, Md.: Grypon House, 1981.
    A collection of recipes for children with an introduction for teachers and parents on values, techniques, and notes of steps in the cooking process best done by adults.

Barrett, Patricia, and Rosemary Dalton. **The Kid's Cookbook.** Concord, Calif.: Nitty Gritty Productions, 1973.
    Excellent cookbook for children. Simple recipes with easy to follow instructions.

Better Homes and Gardens Kids' Snacks. Des Moines, Iowa: Meredith Corporation, 1985.
    A collection of recipes for nutritious snacks. Photographs of the prepared snacks make the preparation of the recipes very appealing.

Better Homes and Gardens Step-By-Step Kids' Cook Book. Des Moines, Iowa: Meredith Corporation, 1984.
    An excellent first cookbook for school-age children. Photographs and step-by-step recipes make cooking easy.

116 / RESOURCES

Bruno, Janet, and Peggy Dakan. **Cooking in the Classroom.** Belmont, Calif.: Pitman, 1974.
A small collection of simple recipes for children.

Cauley, Lorinda Bryan. **Pease-Porridge Hot: A Mother Goose Cookbook.** Lyndhurst, N.J.: Putnam's Sons, 1977.
A collection of recipes inspired by familiar stories and nursery rhymes. Use to extend the enjoyment and understanding of these selected fairy tales and rhymes.

Cooper, Terry T., and Marilyn Ratner. **Many Hands Cooking: An International Cookbook for Girls and Boys.** Illustrated by Tony Chen. New York: Crowell, 1974.
Beautifully illustrated cookbook with recipes from other lands.

Edge, Nellie, comp. **Kids in the Kitchen.** Illustrated by Pierre M. Leitz. Port Angeles, Wash.: Peninsula Publishing, 1975.
Easy recipes for children. Ingredients and measurements for recipes are illustrated in rebus style. Cooking required and no cooking required recipes are included. Nonreaders find the recipes easy to follow.

Faggella, Kathy. **Concept Cookery: Learning Concepts Through Cooking.** Illustrated by Debby Dixler. Bridgeport, Conn.: First Teacher Press, 1985.
Recipes are presented in words and pictures easy for young school-age children to follow. Cooking experiences help children learn concepts in a number of curriculum areas. A section on cooking as an extension of children's literature is included.

Forte, Imogene. **Cookbook: A No-Cook Cook & Learn Book.** Nashville, Tenn.: Incentive Publications, 1983.
Nutritious recipes that children who read can easily follow. No-cook recipes allow more frequent opportunities for cooking with children.

Foster, Florence P., comp. **Adventures in Cooking.** Westfield, N.J.: New Jersey Association for the Education of Young Children, 1971.
A collection of recipes for use in nursery school, day care centers, Head Start programs, kindergartens, and primary classrooms. Good, usable recipes.

Johnson, Barbara, and Betty Plemmons. **Cup Cooking.** Lake Alfred, Fla.: Early Educators Press, 1978.
Individual child portion recipes that even nonreaders can follow independently.

Veitch, Beverly, and Thelma Harms. **Cook and Learn.** Reading, Mass.: Addison-Wesley, 1981.
A collection of single portion recipes. Pictorial directions allow children to independently use each recipe.

Warren, Jean. **Super Snacks.** Alderwood Manor, Wash.: Warren, 1982.
A no sugar, no honey, no artificial sweeteners recipe book for snacks children can prepare. Nutritious snacks suggested for each month of the year.

SPECIAL DAY CELEBRATIONS

Barth, Edna. **Hearts, Cupids, and Red Roses.** Illustrated by Ursula Arndt. New York: Clarion, 1974.
The history of Valentine's Day and the little-known stories behind the symbols are included.

_____. **Lilies, Rabbits, and Painted Eggs.** Illustrated by Ursula Arndt. New York: Clarion, 1970.
  A collection of stories and factual information behind the Easter customs and symbols.

_____. **Shamrocks, Harps, and Shillelaghs.** Illustrated by Ursula Arndt. New York: Clarion, 1977.
  A collection of stories and information on the origin and meaning of the symbols for St. Patrick's Day.

_____. **Turkeys, Pilgrims, and Indian Corn.** Illustrated by Ursula Arndt. New York: Clarion, 1975.
  A collection of stories and factual information on the Thanksgiving symbols and celebration.

_____. **Witches, Pumpkins, and Grinning Ghosts.** Illustrated by Ursula Arndt. New York: Clarion, 1972.
  A collection of stories and information about the Halloween symbols.

Burns, Marilyn. **The Hanukkah Book.** Illustrated by Martha Weston. New York: Four Winds, 1981.
  A complete book about Hanukkah. Information on how and why Hanukkah is celebrated plus traditional and new ways to celebrate the holiday. Hanukkah foods and instructions on making dreidels, different kinds of menorahs, cards, favors, and gifts are included. An excellent resource for planning activities for a Hanukkah unit.

Forte, Imogene. **Holidays: Special Ways to Celebrate Special Days.** Nashville, Tenn.: Incentive Publications, 1983.
  Creative suggestions to help children celebrate the usual holidays.

Giblin, James C. **Fireworks, Picnics, and Flags.** Illustrated by Ursula Arndt. New York: Clarion, 1983.
  The story and history behind the Fourth of July symbols.

Harelson, Randy. **The Kids' Diary of 365 Amazing Days.** New York: Workman, 1979.
  Presents a daily calendar of occasions, historical events, and miscellaneous celebrations, each accompanied by suggested activities. Intended for each child to have a copy. Ideas could be adapted for use with a group.

Hass, C. B. **The Big Book of Recipes for Fun.** Northfield, Ill.: cbh Publishing, 1980.
  A variety of creative learning activities including art, science, cooking, and games. Holiday ideas especially useful.

Lipson, Greta. **It's a Special Day.** Illustrated by Susan Kropa and Wallace Swanson. Carthage, Ill.: Good Apple, 1978.
  A collection of children's poems on special days with background information for teachers and follow-up activities for early elementary school children. Includes ideas for special days during the school year (September through June). Some extra fun ideas that can be used during the summer are also included.

Myers, Robert J. **Celebrations: The Complete Book of American Holidays.** New York: Doubleday, 1972.
  An information book about major holidays, secular and religious, observed in the United States. It helps answer some of the questions school-age children have regarding holidays and religious observances.

Newmann, Dana. **The Early Childhood Teacher's Almanack: Activities for Every Month of the Year.** West Nyack, N.Y.: Center for Applied Research in Education, 1984.

    A valuable collection of unique, practical ideas and suggestions for teachers planning programs for young children. Ideas for field trips, recipes, classroom environments, arts and crafts, and games are presented by the month to reinforce holiday and other special day activities.

Wilmes, Liz, and Wilmes, Dick. **The Circle Time Book.** Dundee, Ill.: Building Blocks, 1982.

    A resource of games, poems, suggested children's literature titles and other activities for holidays and other occasions throughout the year. Excellent resource for planning literature related activities.

INDEX

Aardema, Verna, 44
Abraham Lincoln, 84
Activities
   collections, 35
   magic, 35
   parade, 50, 57
   picnic, 71
   whistling, 56
Adams, Adrienne, 50, 89
Aleichem, Sholom, 60
Aliki, 60
All in a Day, 77
"Alligators All Around," 54
Alphabet books, 31, 54, 69
Amahl and the Night Visitors, 102
American Indian Day, 96-97
American Indians, 29-30, 96-97
Ancona, George, 17, 55
Anderson, Joan, 17, 55
Andy: That's My Name, 20
Angelina on Stage, 46
Animals, 34. See also Birds; Insects
   bears, 43, 46, 75
   chameleons, 27
   dogs, 56
   donkeys, 45
   foxes, 20, 24
   goats, 43
   groundhogs, 84
   horses, 96
   mice, 27, 42
   monkeys, 47, 69
   pigs, 44
   rabbits, 27, 45, 68, 72, 89-90
   wolves, 54
Anno, Mitsumasa, 77
April Foolers, 89
April Fool's Day, 88-89
Arbor Day, 90
Archambault, John, 56
Are You My Mother? 45
Arndt, Ursula, 87

Arrow to the Sun, 29
Arthur's Christmas Cookies, 67, 102
Arthur's Halloween Costume, 98
Asch, Frank, 61
Ask Mr. Bear, 46

Bangs, Edward, 18, 50
Barn Dance! 56
Baskin, Lisa, 69
Beat the Drum: Independence Day Has Come, 93
Bee My Valentine! 84
Bemelmans, Ludwig, 61
Ben's Trumpet, 53
Best Present Is Me, 95
Bible stories, 34, 41, 80, 100
Biggest Bear, 75
Bileck, Marvin, 32, 72
Birds, 45
   chickens, 20, 24, 42-43, 45, 56, 71
   crows, 37, 81
Birthday for Frances, 68, 94
Birthdays, 94-95
Blair, Susan, 43
Blueberries for Sal, 71
Brave Irene, 74
Bread and Jam for Frances, 68
Breads, 42, 68, 71
   corn bread, 60-61
   currant buns, 72
   French toast, 61
   gingerbread, 43, 67
   hot cross buns, 70, 89
   Indian bread, 61
   soda bread, 87
Brett, Jan, 62, 97, 102
Brian Wildsmith's Circus, 58
Briggs, Raymond, 77
Brock, Emma, 70
Brooks, Ron, 77
Brown, Marcia, 19, 42-43, 57, 62
Brown, Margaret Wise, 45

Bruno Munari's ABC, 31
Brustlein, Janice, 78
Bunting, Eve, 62, 97

Cake
   carrot, 68-69
   ginger, 74
   johnny cakes, 70
   king's, 80
   poppy seed, 64
   upside-down, 73, 89
Calvi, Gian, 77
Candy
   haystacks, 72
   honey balls, 63
   maple sugar, 75
Cantwell, Mary, 87
Caps for Sale, 47
Careers, 95
Carle, Eric, 19, 53, 62-63, 77, 94
Carousel, 55
Carrot Cake, 68
Carson, Carol Devine, 30
Cavognaro, David, 63, 97
Cavognaro, Maggie, 63, 97
Cendrars, Blaise, 19
Chair for My Mother, 37, 91
Chanticleer and the Fox, 20
Charles Perrault Day, 83
Chicken Soup with Rice: A Book About Months, 73
Child, Lydia Maria, 50, 99
Chinese New Year, 82-83
Christmas, 22, 41, 51, 67-68, 100-104
Christmas Cat, 102
Christmas Pageant, 41, 100
Cinderella, 43, 57
Circles, Triangles, and Squares, 24
Circus, 58
Clark, Margery, 64
Cohen, Carol, 84
Color of His Own, 27
Concepts
   ABCs, 31, 69
   colors, 24-27, 34
   counting, 50-51, 54, 102
   months of the year, 54, 73, 80
   shapes, 24
   signs, 24
   symbols, 24

Cookies
   butter, 62
   giant birthday, 63
   gingerbread, 67
   monster, 73
   pumpkin, 63
   snowballs, 74
Cooney, Barbara, 20, 23
Corn Is Maize: The Gift of the Indians, 60
Craig, Helen, 46
Cranberry Thanksgiving, 66, 99
Crash! Bang! Boom! 54
Creative dramatics
   puppet shows, 46
   theater, 46
Credle, Ellis, 64
Crews, Donald, 55
Crow Boy, 37, 81
Crowns, 80

Daddy Is a Monster ... Sometimes, 92
Dance
   ballet, 56
   square dance, 57
   waltz, 57
D'Aulaire, Edgar, 64, 84, 86
D'Aulaire, Ingri, 64, 84, 86
Day the Teacher Went Bananas, 69
De Paola, Tomie, 20-21, 41, 65, 80, 85, 93, 100
De Regniers, Beatrice Schenk, 45, 65
Devlin, Harry, 66, 99
Devlin, Wende, 66, 99
Dillon, Diane, 44, 77
Dillon, Leo, 44, 77
Domanska, Janina, 66
Donkey-Donkey, 45
Down, Down the Mountain, 64
Dragons, 30, 82
Dreams, 25
Drummer Hoff, 53
Duvoisin, Roger A., 36, 45, 74, 90

Early American life, 17-19, 23, 32, 55, 72
Easter, 89-90
Easter Egg Artist, 89
Easter eggs, 89
Eastman, P. D., 45
Emberley, Barbara, 21, 51, 53
Emberley, Ed, 21, 51, 53
Ets, Marie Hall, 22, 88, 100

Fables, 42
Family life
  babies, 51
  fathers, 92-93
  grandparents, 95-96
  mothers, 37, 45-46, 71, 91-92
Family tree, 96
Farm, 23-24, 51, 56-57, 67, 88
Farmer in the Dell, 51
Father's Day, 92-93
Feelings, Muriel, 55
Feelings, Tom, 55
Fisher, Aileen, 104
Flack, Marjorie, 46
Flag Day, 92
Flags, 35, 57, 87, 92
Folk and fairy tales, 19, 29-30, 42-44, 66-67, 70-71, 83-84
Foods. *See also* Cake; Candy; Cookies; Soup
  apples, 32-33
  applesauce, 32, 72
  bananas, 69-70
  blueberries, 71
  carrots, 68
  cherries, 64
  corn, 60
  cranberries, 66, 99
  eggs, 68, 74
  ham, 74
  honey, 62
  hot chocolate, 68
  ice cream, 70-71
  jam, 68, 71
  lemonade, 61
  pancakes, 60, 65, 70-71
  pasta, 65
  pizza, 65
  popcorn, 21, 65
  pumpkin, 97-98
  squash, 67
  turnips, 64, 66
Foreign lands, 77-78
  Africa, 19, 44-45, 55-56
  China, 30-31, 82-83
  France, 61
  India, 42
  Japan, 37, 81-82
  Mexico, 22, 88, 100
  Russia, 64
Foster, Mariana Curtis, 78
Frederick, 27
Freeman, Don, 22, 89
Friends, 27, 45, 65

Gage, Wilson, 67
Galdone, Paul, 42, 67, 71
George Washington, 64, 86-87
Giant Jam Sandwich, 71
Gilberto and the Wind, 22, 88
Gingerbread Boy, 67
Ginsburg, Mirra, 23
Girl Who Loved Wild Horses, 96
Goble, Paul, 96
Goffstein, M. B., 56
Good Lemonade, 61
Goode, Diane, 32, 72
Graham, Margaret B., 38, 88
Grandparents' Day, 95-96
Green Eggs and Ham, 74
Groundhog Day, 84
Guilfoile, Elizabeth, 46

Hafner, Marilyn, 91, 98
Hall, Donald, 23
Halloween, 26, 46-47, 97-99
Hannukah, 60, 104-6
Hanukah Money, 60
Happy Mother's Day, 91
Harold and the Purple Crayon, 25
Hats, 18
Hayashi, Akiko, 77
Hazen, Barbara, 53
Henry's Fourth of July, 93
Hide and Seek Fog, 36
Hirsh, Marilyn, 104
Hoban, Lillian, 67-69, 84, 94, 98, 102
Hoban, Russell, 68, 94
Hoban, Tana, 24
Hogrogain, Nonny, 68
Holarbird, Katharine, 46
Holidays
  American Indian Day, 96-97
  April Fool's Day, 88-89
  Arbor Day, 90
  Charles Perrault Day, 83
  Chinese New Year, 82-83
  Christmas, 22, 41, 51, 67-68, 100-104
  Easter, 89-90
  Father's Day, 92-93
  Flag Day, 92
  Grandparents' Day, 95-96
  Groundhog Day, 84
  Halloween, 26, 46-47, 97-99
  Hanukkah, 60, 104-6
  Independence Day, 18, 50, 71, 93-94
  Japanese New Year, 37, 81
  Labor Day, 95

Holidays (*continued*)
  Mother's Day, 37, 91-92
  New Year's Day, 77-80
  Presidents' birthdays
    Lincoln, Abraham, 84
    Washington, George, 64, 86-87
  St. Patrick's Day, 62, 87
  Thanksgiving, 50, 66, 99-100
  Valentine's Day, 22, 30, 84-86
Holmes, Efner Tudor, 102
Honeybee and the Robber, 62
Hopkins, Lee Bennett, 93
Hosea, Tobias, 69
Hosea's Alphabet, 69
Hot Cross Buns and Other Old Street Cries, 70, 89
House That Jack Built, 57
Howe, James, 69
Hurd, Clement, 45
Hush, Little Baby, 51
Hutchins, Pat, 24, 56

I Know an Old Lady Who Swallowed a Fly, 50
I Love Hanukkah, 104
I See a Song, 53
Illustration techniques
  collage, 26-28
  marbleizing, 25
  scratch board, 20
  watercolor, 22-23, 26, 28, 35, 37
  woodcut, 21-22
In a Dark, Dark Room and Other Scary Stories, 46
Independence Day, 18, 50, 71, 93-94
Insects
  fireflies, 36
  flies, 50
  mosquitoes, 44
  spiders, 19
Instruments, musical, 54
  drums, 51, 53, 55, 58
  fiddle, 56-57
  harmonica, 57
  trumpet, 53
  violin, 54
Is It Red? Is It Yellow? Is It Blue? 24
Isadora, Rachel, 53, 65
It Looked Like Spilt Milk, 34
It's Halloween, 98

Jacobs, Joseph, 70
Johnny-Cake, 70
Johnny Maple-Leaf, 36, 90

Johnson, Crockett, 25
Joseph and His Brothers, 42

Kandell, Alice, 58
Keats, Ezra Jack, 25-26, 46, 51, 56, 94
Keller, Holly, 93
Kellogg, Steven, 18, 50
Kiedrowski, Priscilla, 104
Kites, 22, 81, 88
Kroll, Steven, 91

Labor Day, 95
Langstaff, John, 70, 89
Leaves, 36, 90
Lent, Blair, 30, 82
Lentil, 57
Let's Make Rabbits, 27, 89
Letter to Amy, 94
Lexau, Joan, 70
Lionni, Leo, 27-28, 89
Lindvall, Ella K., 42
Literature based activities
  celebrations, 76-106
    evaluation, 77
    objectives, 11
    techniques, 77
    values, 76
  cooking, 59-75
    evaluation, 60
    objectives, 11
    techniques, 77
    values, 59
  creative art, 16-38
    evaluation, 17
    objectives, 11
    techniques, 17
    values, 16
  creative dramatics, 39-47
    evaluation, 41
    literature for, 40
    objectives, 11
    techniques, 40
    values, 39
  music, 48-58
    evaluation, 49
    literature for, 49
    objectives, 11
    techniques, 48
    values, 48

Literature based programming
  guidelines, 13
  objectives, 10-11
  rationale, 9
Little Bear's New Year's Party, 78
"Little Boy Blue," 72
Little Drummer Boy, 51
"Little Miss Muffet," 72
Little Red Hen, 71
Little Red Riding Hood, 42
Little Shubert, 56
Little Yellow, Little Blue, 27
Lobel, Arnold, 31
Lord, John Vernon, 71
Louie, 46

Madeline, 61
Madeline's Rescue, 61
Majo Means One, 55
Maps, 24
Martin, Bill, Jr., 56
Marzollo, Jean, 30
Maurice Sendak's Really Rosie, 54
Max, the Music Maker, 58
May I Bring a Friend? 45, 65
Mayer, Mercer, 46
McCloskey, Robert, 57, 71
McCully, Emily, 23, 71
McDermott, Gerald, 29
McKie, Roy, 88
Menotti, Gian Carlo, 102
Merry Christmas: Children at Christmastime Around the World, 103
Molan, Chris, 42
Monsters, 23, 33, 47, 57, 73
Montresor, Beni, 45, 65
Moodie, John, 36
Mosel, Arlene, 30, 82
Mother Goose. *See* Nursery rhymes
Mother's Day, 37, 91-92
Mountain life, 17, 32, 72
Müller, Jörg, 54
Munari, Bruno, 31
My First Hanukkah Book, 104

Names, 20-21, 37
New Year's Day, 77-80
Nine Days to Christmas, 22, 100
Noah's Ark, 21, 34, 51
Noah's Ark, 34
Nobody Listens to Andrew, 46
Nursery rhymes, 44, 52, 72

Oechsli, Kelly, 73, 89
Oh, Were They Ever Happy! 35
Once a Mouse, 42
"One Was Johnny," 54
One Wide River to Cross, 21, 51
Ookie-Spooky, 23
Opening Night, 56
Over the River and Through the Wood, 50, 99
Ox-Cart Man, 23

Pancakes for Breakfast, 65
Parker, Nancy Winslow, 70, 89
Peek, Merle, 51
Peppe, Rodney, 57
Perrault, Charles, 43, 57, 83-84
Peter and the Wolf, 54
Peter Spier's Rain, 57
Petersham, Maud, 64
Petersham, Miska, 64
Picnic, 71
Pioneer Children of Appalachia, 17, 55
Poetry, 31-32
Popcorn Book, 21, 65
Popov, Nicolai Ye., 77
Poppy Seed Cakes, 64
Potter, Beatrix, 72
Prelutsky, Jack, 31, 98
Presidents' birthdays
  Lincoln, Abraham, 84
  Washington, George, 64, 86-87
Programming guide uses, 11-12
  child care teachers, 12
  children's librarians, 12
  classroom teachers, 12
Prokofiev, Sergei, 54
Psst! Doggie, 56
Pumpkin People, 63, 97

Rain Makes Applesauce, 32, 72
Rainbow of My Own, 22
Rand, Ted, 56
Random House Book of Poetry for Children, 31
Really Spring, 38, 88
Rebus Treasury, 30
Recipes, 23, 60-74
Regards to the Man in the Moon, 25
Resolutions, 79
Riddle Book, 88
Riddles, 88
Roll Over! A Counting Song, 51
Rosie's Walk, 24, 56

Rounds, Glen, 67
Runaway Bunny, 45

Sandwich, 71
Scary, Scary Halloween, 97
Scarry, Richard, 95
Schaaf, Peter, 54
Scheer, Julian, 32, 72-73, 89
School-age child care, programming
  activities, 6-8
  facilities, 6
  field trips, 8, 32, 54-56, 72, 82, 84, 88, 90, 92, 94-97
  group management, 8
  group size, 8-9
  interest centers, 6-8
    arts and crafts, 7
    blocks and construction, 7
    books, 6
    cooking, 7
    creative dramatics, 7
    games and puzzles, 7
    music, 7
    science, 7
  schedule, 6
  staff, 8
School-age child care, programs
  models, 5-6
    adult centered, 5
    child centered, 5
    unit based, 5-6, 13-15
School-age children
  characteristics, 1-2
    five-year-old, 1
    six-year-old, 2
    seven-year-old, 2
    eight-year-old, 2
  developmental tasks, 2-3
  interests, 3-5
    assessment, 3
    questionnaire, 4
Schwartz, Alvin, 46
Sea life, 28-29
Seasons, 23, 35-36, 38
  fall, 35-36, 83
  spring, 31, 38, 88
  winter, 36
Secret Birthday Message, 63, 94
Secret codes, 55, 94
Sendak, Maurice, 33-34, 47, 54, 57, 73
Seuss, Dr., 74
Shadow, 19
Shadows, 19-20, 84

Shaw, Charles, 34
Shulevitz, Uri, 60
Simont, Marc, 36, 90
Slobodkina, Esphyr, 47
Snow Day, 25
Songs
  animal, 51-52
  Christmas, 52, 102-3
  folk, 50-52, 55
  nursery rhymes, 52
  patriotic, 50, 53
  Thanksgiving, 50
Sorcerer's Apprentice, 53
Soup
  alphabet, 69
  chicken and rice, 73
  stone, 19, 62
  vegetable, 62
Space, 25
Spier, Peter, 34-35, 54, 57, 92
Squash Pie, 67
St. Patrick's Day, 62, 87
St. Patrick's Day, 87
St. Patrick's Day in the Morning, 62
Star-Spangled Banner, 35, 57, 92
Stecher, Miriam, 58
Steig, William, 34, 74
Steptoe, John, 92
Steven Kellogg's Yankee Doodle, 18, 50
Stevens, Mary, 46
Stone Soup, 19, 62
Stones, 19, 35
Story of the Three Wise Kings, 41, 80, 100
Strega Nona, 65
Striped Ice Cream, 70
Swimmy, 28
Sylvester and the Magic Pebble, 35

Thanksgiving, 50, 66, 99-100
Thayer, Marjorie, 89
Things to Make and Do for Valentine's Day, 85
This Old Man, 50
Thousand Lights and Fireflies, 36
Three Billy Goats Gruff, 43
Tikki Tikki Tembo, 30, 82
Treasury of Peter Rabbit and Other Stories, 72
Tree Is Nice, 36-37, 90
Trees, 36-37, 90
Tresselt, Alvin, 36, 74, 90
Trip, 26
Troll, 43
Tudor, Tasha, 102

Turkle, Brinton, 50, 99
Turnip, 66
Twelve Days of Christmas, 102

Udry, Janice May, 36, 90
Ungerer, Tomi, 53
Unit/themes
   American Indians, 29-30, 96-97
   apples, 32-33, 65, 72
   author/illustrator studies
      Carle, Eric, 19, 53, 62-63, 77, 94
      Hoban, Tana, 24
      Keats, Ezra Jack, 25-26, 46
      Lionni, Leo, 27-28, 89
      Perrault, Charles, 43, 57, 83-84
      Sendak, Maurice, 33-34, 47, 54, 57, 73
   bananas, 69-70
   Christmas, 22, 41, 51, 100-104
   colors/color combinations, 22, 24-25, 27-28, 35
   early American life, 17-19, 23, 32, 55
   Easter, 27, 45, 68, 72, 89-90
   fall, 32, 35-37, 72-73, 90
   fathers, 92-93
   folk and fairy tales, 19, 29-30, 42-44, 66-67, 70-71, 83-84
   foreign lands, 37-38
      Africa, 19, 44-45, 55-56
      China, 30-31, 82-83
      Japan, 37, 81-82
   grandparents, 95-96
   Halloween, 19, 26, 46-47, 97-99
   Hanukkah, 60, 104-6
   Independence Day, 18, 50, 71, 93-94
   monsters, 23, 33, 47, 57, 73
   mothers, 37, 45-46, 71, 91-92
   musical instruments, 51-54
   new year, 77-83
   nursery rhymes, 44, 52, 72
   rabbits, 27, 45, 68, 72, 89-90
   safety, 95
   sea life, 28-29
   shadows, 19, 84
   spring, 31, 35-38, 88
   stones, 19, 35
   Valentine's, 22, 30, 84-86
Upside Down Day, 73, 89

Wake Up, Groundhog! 84
Ward, Lynd, 75
Weather
   clouds, 34
   fog, 36
   rain, 32, 57
   rainbows, 22
   snow, 25-26, 36, 74
   snowflakes, 25-26
   wind, 22, 88
What Do People Do All Day? 95
When I Was Young in the Mountains, 32, 72
Where the Wild Things Are, 33, 47, 57, 73
Whistle for Willie, 56
White Snow, Bright Snow, 36, 74
Why Mosquitoes Buzz in People's Ears, 44
Wildsmith, Brian, 58
Williams, Vera B., 37, 91
Wilson, Robina B., 103
Wise men, 41, 80, 100
Wolf, Janet, 95

Yashima, Taro, 37, 81
You're the Scaredy Cat, 46

Zemach, Margot, 51
Zhu, Chengliang, 77
Zimmer, Dirk, 46
Zimmerman, Marie, 61
Zion, Gene, 38, 88
Zuromskis, Diane, 51